Lou Manfredini's
Kitchen Smarts

How to renovate, repair, and maintain the most-used room in your home

Lou Manfredini's
Kitchen Smarts

How to renovate, repair, and maintain the most-used room in your home

Lou Manfredini
with Curtis Rist

Ballantine Books
New York

A Ballantine Book
Published by The Random House Publishing Group

Copyright © 2004 by Lou Manfredini
Illustrations copyright © 2004 by Harry Trumbore

www.ballantinebooks.com

LIBRARY OF CONGRESS CATALOGING-IN-PUBLICATION DATA

ISBN 0-345-44988-6

Text design by Michaelis/Carpelis Design Assoc. Inc.

Manufactured in the United States of America

First Edition: May 2004

10 9 8 7 6 5 4 3 2 1

Acknowledgments

Think back to a Julia Child cooking show, and the impression you're left with is of one person hard at work, in love with the task at hand. Behind the camera, however, is a whole roomful of people who make that possible—people you don't necessarily see, but who are the essential ingredients in a foolproof recipe. In a way, that's how I feel writing this book. Turn the camera away from me, and you would find a collection of some of the smartest people in publishing, who also happen to be some of the kindest and quickest-witted people on the planet, giving me an assist.

You would find my wife and manager, Mary Beth Manfredini, and my agent Brian DeFiore. Curtis Rist, the greatest co-author on Earth would be there, as would Harry Trumbore, our illustrator. Kathy Neumeyer would be standing by, her researcher's bearing fully intact, as would Maureen O'Neal, our editor at Ballantine Books. Beyond them would be a crowd of people who helped keep this book simmering through the long and delicate process of creation, including Ballantine's editorial and production staff. Their generosity with deadlines and genius with editing suggestions made this book a joy to write—and, I hope, to read.

Lou Manfredini

Contents

Introduction   ix

Chapter 1: A Design in Mind   3

Which would you prefer—a lifestyle that suits your kitchen,
or a kitchen that suits your lifestyle?

Chapter 2: Cabinet Fever!   25

Storage, more than any other element, defines the kitchen; all good design
plans begin here.

Chapter 3: Counter Intelligence   49

Here's the recipe for creating a hardworking surface that looks great.

Chapter 4: Pipe Dreams   71

Here's everything you need to know about plumbing—
including the kitchen sink.

Chapter 5: Lighten Up!   89

With a combination of natural and electric lighting,
even an ordinary kitchen can have a bright future.

Chapter 6: Mechanical Inclinations   111

A ventilation system and major appliances form the
mechanical core of the kitchen.

Appendix: Essential Resources   131

Not sure where to turn to find out more about your
kitchen-to-be? Let the journey begin here. Plus planning grids.

Introduction

Friends of mine named Steve and Jane have a house they didn't much like. While the place looked inviting enough, with its broad front porch, quaintly weathered shingles, and spacious living room downstairs, the kitchen was another matter. The white Formica countertops had become pocked with about three decades' worth of chop marks and burn marks from pots. The enameled sink, with its rust stains and ugly chips, looked like something from *The Grapes of Wrath*. And although the golden oak cabinets weren't bad, the faded Peter Max–style flower door pulls that adorned them turned the whole thing into a farce. "I can't quite put my finger on what's wrong here, but I really can't stand this place," said Jane, with some understatement. "It's all the kitchen's fault."

No surprise there. As Americans, we spend about 80 percent of our waking hours in the kitchen. Just think for a moment, and make a brief list of what we do here. We clean up, we feed the dog and cat, we post notes for our kids and leave telephone messages for our spouse, we talk on the phone, we sort the garbage, we balance our checkbook, and, oh yes, we occasionally even make a sandwich. That's just for starters. In most households, the kitchen also becomes the homework command center on school nights, the location of choice for informal get-togethers, and the place where we brainstorm ideas with family and friends or just kick back and have a good time. If you think about it, the focus of any holiday meal shouldn't be the dining room table; it should be the kitchen, where the true spirit of a family working together can be found. If a kitchen vexes you, either because of a dated décor or a long list of things that just don't work right, it wouldn't matter if you lived in a mansion. You're still going to hate your house.

I can show you a way to create a better home life by giving you the specific knowledge you need to help create a kitchen you can live with, at a price you can afford. There are plenty of books out there doling out mind-numbing step-by-step instructions about how to install a sink or replace a faucet—but they don't add up to anything that can help you create the overall vision you need to confidently craft a kitchen you'll love. At the same time, there are countless showcase kitchens in books and magazines that will have you yearning for finished details such as quarter-sawn oak flooring and handmade Arts and Crafts backsplashes, but they won't necessarily empower you to create a list of projects that will form the basis of a solid room that will last. By showing you the essential elements to consider in any renovation, whether it is a $1,000 weekend makeover or a $100,000 showstopper, I can give you the recipe you need for kitchen success.

Approaching a kitchen renovation with wisdom is essential, partly because the amount of money people spend runs so high. The average cost of a kitchen remodeling project now runs between an astounding $40,000 and $70,000, according to the National Association of the Remodeling Industry. Yet this dollar amount represents only part of the cost, since renovating a kitchen requires a huge investment in terms of time and aggravation, as well. How are you going to cook for your family, for instance, if your kitchen is nothing but a cave of exposed joists and studs for a few months during construction? You can't just sit down one morning and say, "I think I'll redo the kitchen today," the way you might suddenly decide to wallpaper the hallway; the whole process requires forethought and strategy.

That's where this book fits in. I can't dictate what style I think you should choose, or whether to go with the overlay or inset cabinet doors. These are ultimately matters of personal taste. But I can help you come up with a plan for getting it right, no matter your preference or budget. You could put in $10,000 worth of granite countertops, but what's the point if they are tilted in a way that spills immediately onto the floor? You could install a fancy double sink hand-chiseled out of soapstone, but where will the satisfaction be if you have to listen to one sink gurgle and cough while the other one drains? Fine, go ahead and tile the floor with Brazilian slate you handpicked from the quarry, but who's going to "ooh" and "ahh" if it all starts to crack and bust up because of a squishy sub-floor that somehow didn't figure into your design plans?

I will not be talking about a lot of hard-to-comprehend projects, but will instead focus on universal things to keep in mind that apply to every kitchen in the country, such as cabinets, countertops, floors, plumbing, appliances, and the best ways to bring in natural as well as electric lighting. I will show you what projects you can do yourself, and what projects I think will require an expert's assistance. I can't predict the actual cost of the materials and labor involved in your project, but I can give you some guidelines about what I think they should cost in relation to your overall budget. Think of this as a field guide to a kitchen renovation, based on my twenty years of making the right (and, more instructively, the wrong) choices as a professional builder.

My friends Steve and Jane followed my approach to come up with a plan that worked for them. Instead of moving entirely or spending $80,000 on a gut renovation, they took a streamlined yet no less transforming approach. Out went the ugly countertops, the sink, the faucet, the "grandma" vinyl flooring, and those precious flowered door pulls. In went new countertops, a prefinished wood flooring system, a new sink, and updated brushed-nickel cabinet hardware. They had a contractor correct a few problems they hadn't even known about, such as an antiquated exhaust system. When it was all done, topped off by a few gallons of carefully applied paint, the kitchen was reborn. "I love the new kitchen, and what's even better is that now I love this house, too," says Jane, of the project that cost—ready for this?—just $7,380.

I can't promise you a cost-savings success such as this. But I can promise that by following the projects I detail on the coming pages you will learn all you need to create a kitchen that satisfies you more than just superficially. No matter how modest or how grand your vision might be, you're going to be cooking, and living, in style.

Lou Manfredini's
Kitchen Smarts

How to renovate, repair, and maintain the most-used room in your home

chapter ONE

A Design in Mind

Which would you prefer— a lifestyle that suits your kitchen, or a kitchen that suits your lifestyle?

A few years ago, an acquaintance of mine named Phil bought a modest 1960s ranch in Los Angeles and tried to update it by adding the most lavish kitchen he could imagine. "I heard it's the number one way to increase the value of a home," he said. "Anything that I spend here, I'll double when I go to sell."

Phil's spend-anything approach, however, quickly got him into trouble. He knocked out one wall and built a giant glass lean-to for the breakfast table, the kind you now see at every Burger King. This "bigger is better" approach led to a room that measures about 30 feet from one end to the other, and is done entirely in white. If you stand at one end of the kitchen, you literally have to call out loud to be heard at the other end. Rather than a kitchen, it looks more like something from the bridge of *Star Trek*'s *Enterprise*. The price tag also had an element of science fiction to it: $95,000. Worse still, when he tried to sell the place eight years after this misguided renovation, the real estate agent told him something a homeowner dreads most of all. "I'm still in shock," Phil said with a sputter on the telephone. "She told me the kitchen was *dated.*"

Now, a lot of things can go wrong with a house. You can discover the

entire structure has been eaten by termites, for instance, or find you're located on the right-of-way for a new highway. But worse than either of these would be to spend $95,000 on a kitchen, only to have it turn sour as old milk before a decade is out. Yet this is a risk we homeowners face. Our houses have gotten larger and larger over the years, but rather than spreading out our various activities through the whole house, we seem to concentrate them in the kitchen. There's no more dynamic, essential room in any home. Naturally, there is a tendency to overdo things, to somehow attempt to create a kitchen that tries to live up to someone else's fantasy of what the room should be, rather than living up to your own unique needs, wishes, and quirks. Instead, I think the goal should be to create a room that suits your needs and gives you comfort and convenience every day you live in your home. By its very functionality, rather than its show-off attempt at style, your kitchen will become a selling point when you choose to move.

Designers offer a thousand rules about how to attain this and about what a kitchen should be, in terms of layout and measurements. While some of this is helpful as a guide, I prefer to think of it as just that: a guide. Instead, your kitchen should emerge as a product of your own vision, the realities of your own lifestyle, and the even starker constraints of your own budget. Sure, adding a lavish kitchen often makes good financial sense in terms of the long-term value of your house—as long as you don't go overboard. Yet even if you don't have the $40,000 to $70,000 you would need to do a total renovation, you can benefit from following the same steps during a far more modest makeover. Let's start with the basics of design, which will help you no matter how modest or lavish your plans might be.

A Place to Start

If designing a kitchen involved nothing more than figuring out where the cabinets should go and chucking a counter on top, everybody's job would be easy. Especially mine. There's much more to it than this, however—which will still come as a surprise to many builders and do-it-yourselfers across the country who opt for shortcuts. Doing a kitchen right involves paying attention to a few basic elements.

To me, the most important element of a kitchen, like the most important element in real estate, is location—and in a kitchen, good location has everything to do with good lighting. If you're lucky enough to be able to choose exactly where you can locate the kitchen, the best place for it is with an orientation toward the east or southeast. This will allow the morning sun to fill it with light, which will do far more than the caffeine in your coffee to perk up your family. Of course, in renovating a house, choosing a new location isn't always possible. In this case, a great deal can be done to bring in lighting, through a clever use of new windows and bump-outs, as well as carefully installed electrical lighting. We'll take a more illuminating look at lighting in Chapter 5.

A second major element to consider is traffic. Think of the kitchen as

Steal This Space!

While the cost of renovating a kitchen can mount not just up to but through the ceiling, the cost of adding space to a house in the form of an addition can be through the roof. Even something as simple as a 15-by-10-foot breakfast nook measuring a modest 150 square feet can easily cost $20,000 or more. Instead of adding space, one way to keep costs under control is by stealing space from adjacent rooms. Does your kitchen adjoin a large living room that you seldom use? Consider building a dividing wall to absorb some of the space. Are there any large closets that abut the kitchen in other rooms? Consider taking those over as well; you'll be able to more than compensate for the lost storage space in a well-designed kitchen. Does the kitchen adjoin a mudroom, laundry room, or back entry hall that connects to the garage? Find a way to absorb it into the new kitchen plans. This is a technique that city apartment dwellers have known about for decades, and is a great way to reconfigure the floor plan of your home. The space isn't exactly free, since you still have to erect walls, refinish floors, and finish the interior. But it will cost far less than building an addition from scratch, and you won't have to spend money heating and cooling that additional space.

the Times Square of your home, in the same way that 42nd Street is the Crossroads of the World. It's the place where everyone meets, prepares meals, eats, and simply hangs out. There's always a lot going on here, from dawn until midnight, which means that the more you can cut down on the unnecessary need for people to walk through the kitchen, the better off you'll be. To remedy this, I'm a big proponent of a circular flow of traffic, not just in the kitchen but everywhere in the house. Many traditional homes have a center entry, a living room and dining room to the right and left, and a kitchen to the rear. When you enter, you can make a big loop around the house. What this does is ease the flow of people moving around in a home, so they don't bump into one another.

Although it may seem imperceptible, the home actually becomes more comfortable to live in.

The same should be true of the kitchen itself. If you create a kitchen where people can circulate freely, you'll be a lot more comfortable working in there than in a kitchen where you have to stop and back out to go the other way around someone. Wherever possible, engineer as many entrances and exits to the kitchen as possible. One way to do this, if you're starting from scratch, is to have an entrance from the kitchen to the mudroom or garage. This makes it easier to manage the trash,

Color Me . . . Ridiculous

All right, now I've heard everything. Every decade seems to bring with it an embarrassing palette of colors that go out of fashion as quickly as they come into fashion. In the '50s, there was aqua and a pale sort of Pepto-Bismol pink that found its way to excess on walls and ceramic tiles. In the '60s and '70s, we had appliances decorated in two-tone shades of Harvest Gold and Avocado in just about every house in the country. Well, the color designers are at it again. This time, marketing experts have decided we're in the "blue" decade, only they're not calling it blue. We've now got Blue Aire, for instance, which is based on the metallic shades of '60s cars. Then there's Deep Arctic, which can best be described as sort of a mildewed navy blue. There's even a move to introduce an Avocado-like green that has been rechristened Guacamole, to appeal to a hipper audience. My advice? Follow your taste and your own sense of style, rather than the pretensions of some ad agency that gets paid to put a new name on old colors. Instead of leaping toward colors-of-the-moment, I prefer sticking with the solid durability of natural materials, such as granite, slate, and natural woods. These never go out of fashion. If you crave blue, or even Deep Arctic, great— just be cautious. This will be your kitchen this year, next year, and the year after that. If you choose some color-of-the-moment, you run the risk of ending up with Guacamole on your face.

Go Ahead, Break the Rules

The perfect kitchen can't be distilled to a simple set of rules—the way a recipe for, say, the perfect meatloaf can. Instead, it's the result of trade-offs and choices that produce a room that works best for you, at a price you can afford.

without making a mess in the kitchen, and also relieves some of the clutter. You'll have to pay attention to the natural traffic flow through the kitchen, as well. Here, the goal is to reroute people out of the cooking area, defined as the zone between the kitchen, stove, and refrigerator. Much as you love your family, it can be annoying to jostle into them constantly while you're standing at the stove trying to cook and they're trying to reach into the refrigerator behind you.

Another consideration is the noise generated by a kitchen in full swing. It can get pretty rowdy, especially with pots banging, water rushing, the

Demolition Derby

Let's face it, a full kitchen renovation carries an enormous price tag—$30,000, $40,000, $50,000, and even more. While it takes a great deal of skillful carpentry to pull off a project of this size, there is one aspect of it that anyone can do and save money: the demolition.

When a major renovation begins, the old kitchen has to be gutted, right down to the studs. That means that everything has to go, from the countertops and cabinets to the kitchen sink. This job takes a contractor days, and as you might have guessed, it is not one that involves a lot of finesse. You simply go in there, rip everything out, and in a few days you're done. I've found that the great motivator for this particular project is a box of Ho-Hos and some coffee and maybe a six-pack of beer at the end of the day, which should be more than enough to entice a few buddies over to join in the home wrecking.

There are a few rules needed to keep things under control, however. First, have the contractor explain exactly what to rip out, and how to do it. Since you're eliminating a major headache from his punch list, he'll more than likely go over the details with great eagerness. Second, have him disconnect all the plumbing and electrical connections *before* you start swinging the crowbars. Finally, make a plan beforehand to get rid of everything that you're ripping out, whether it's a Dumpster in the yard, or a borrowed pickup truck to haul everything to the dump. The effort is worth it, believe me. Depending on the size of the project, you could probably save close to $5,000 compared to paying a contractor.

dishwasher churning, the blender and food processor spinning, and a hundred other devices adding their own dissonance. The din from a kitchen can cause a fairly severe culture clash if the kitchen is connected to a family room or great room, where the rest of the family is trying to catch up on something urgent—say, the lost *SpongeBob Squarepants* episodes. While it's possible to build kitchens that connect with family rooms or are located downstairs from the baby's nursery, it has to be done with an awareness of the noise that can be generated. It's often a far easier task to relocate rooms than it is to try to control the din with sound-deadening techniques or to quiet down the family chef.

One last major element everyone confronts when renovating a kitchen is the issue of standard sizes. We all want our kitchens to be unique, and we all also want our kitchens to conform to our budgets. The reality, however, is that we are working for the most part within a certain set of fixed parameters. Countertops are 26 inches deep, for instance, and base cabinets are 34½ inches high. You almost always need 24 inches for a dishwasher, for instance, and you almost always need a 33-inch-wide sink base. Refrigerators, except those found in college dorms, are typically 33 inches wide. If you search hard enough, you can find deviations from these. You can find tiny 18-inch-wide dishwashers and oversized ones that are 30 inches wide, for instance, and you can also find dishwashers that pull out in large cabinet drawers instead of doors. If you

Divide and Conquer

Separate cooktops and ovens have been popular for years, but a "rule" of the kitchen has been that they have to be located in the same spot, as if they were one unit. I think it's time to rewrite this particular rule since they perform two different functions. If you want to have the cooktop that you use constantly in the center of the kitchen, while you move the stove that you use less frequently to an out-of-the-way corner, go ahead and do it. If this flexibility works to your advantage, take it.

have a particular need for an odd-sized appliance, a good contractor will help find them, as well as finding ways to make conventional-sized appliances fit. Just know that any deviations from the standard are going to cost more, and will ultimately leave you less money to spend on upgrades you might have preferred instead.

In addition to conventional appliance dimensions, there are also some standard layout dimensions that should be followed—particularly in regard to the walkway between an island and a row of cabinets adjacent to it. Here, the amount of space needed is deceptively large. While 36 inches makes a great opening for a doorway, it does not give you enough room to work with here. In a 3-foot-wide corridor, you would be continuously bumping into anyone else in the kitchen. In fact, it would require you to become a contortionist simply to open the dishwasher and empty it. The minimum space I would recommend in this case is 42 inches, but 48 inches—that's 4 feet—is even better. And if this is the main corridor in your kitchen, rather than just a side alleyway, I think you need 5 feet to make it work.

Laying on the Layout

Back when George Washington was designing Mt. Vernon, he had a simple approach to designing the kitchen: Place it in a separate building next to the house. That way if it caught fire, as old kitchens invariably did, it wouldn't take the whole house with it. Kitchens have evolved since then, beginning with their move indoors. Even here, they were relegated to the back of the house or someplace inconsequential. Things have surely changed in the last decade or so to the point where now it seems to be the kitchen—not the living room or the dining room—that is the central guest location. We're no longer hiding in there toiling away, suddenly emerging with perfectly roasted crown ribs of beef to dazzle guests *à la* Julia Child. In many cases, our guests are right in there with us helping put together a relaxed yet memorable dinner.

The remarkable thing is the variety of kitchen layouts that are possible

using the space you already have. If you do nothing but prepare food in a kitchen, with no socializing and no more than one or two people in there at any one time, then it's possible to go toward a galley kitchen, which is streamlined and functions simply as a work kitchen. This doesn't mean it has to be ugly, by any means, but its layout and size limit its role in the house. If you want to eat in the kitchen, you can expand the basic galley kitchen slightly to include a stool or two placed by the counter, or around an island or peninsula counter. If you want a larger kitchen with a table or a kitchen that blends into a larger living space or great room, then the configuration has to expand to make room for that.

What's involved in the workings of the kitchen varies, as well. Of course, there are the basics—the refrigerator, sink, and stove, and in many cases a dishwasher. The goal is to configure these things logically, not just so that they conform to some designer's notion of a magic triangle, but to a configuration that works logically for how you use your

Building a Checklist

Sure, we all know what we want in a kitchen—until we actually go and try to describe it to a contractor or designer, whose job it is to help us get it. When they ask us what we do in our kitchen, we end up saying things like, "Well, I use it to cook." If they ask what we dream our kitchen could be, we answer with the even less helpful, "I wish it were nicer." Try to design a kitchen based on that!

Professional designers take a more specific approach to help you communicate your desires in a language they understand. Start by creating a log. Don't just write a wish list of what you want your kitchen to be; the chances are you'll be thinking too narrowly. Instead, start creating a list of the things you do—or would like to do—in your kitchen. Get a notepad and jot down your kitchen activities for three or four days, from cooking to sorting the trash, to hauling groceries, and household repair projects. Did you spend five minutes cooking dinner, or five hours? Did you cook alone, or with help? What else is going on in the kitchen—TV watching, or perhaps a load of laundry? What did you do to prepare dinner, bake and sauté? Or reheat and defrost? Along the way, write down the kinds of things you really would love to do in your kitchen, but can't. This is an essential step that will help you decide what renovations make sense for your space, based on how you use it. Some of your notes may seem obvious at first, but added together they will provide a real insight into the way you want your kitchen to function, in a way no simple description ever will.

Can You Go It Alone?

The boundary between a do-it-yourself project and one that a contractor should handle is about $5,000. Below this, homeowners can successfully handle the demands with a careful approach. Above this, the mistakes they'll make will likely consume any savings.

kitchen. It makes logical sense to put the dishwasher near the sink, of course. But where is the refrigerator? On the opposite side of the kitchen where there's an alcove? Across from the stove so you have easy access to cooking? While I happen to like positioning the sink beneath a window, it doesn't have to go there—it can go anywhere. The choices are limitless, based on what works, as well as the space that you have.

Sizing Things Up

People always ask me how big a kitchen should be, and I always have the same answer: It depends. What kind of cooking do you do, and how are you going to use it? Do you envision the kitchen as the storage depot for everything in your home, the way some people think of attics? Do you buy every new kitchen gadget as soon as the Williams-Sonoma catalog hits your mailbox? If this is the case, you need a hardworking kitchen. On the flip side, there are plenty of people who rarely set foot in their kitchens other than to do a little microwaving or use the telephone to order takeout. Building an excessively large and luxurious kitchen in these cases is a waste of money. Some non-cooks might imagine a kitchen that shrinks to nothing and then disappears into the wall, like a Murphy bed. That's probably too extreme, of course, because even if you don't cook much the kitchen is still the area in your home where everybody expects and wants to congregate. The point is, how you lay out your kitchen should really be based on your lifestyle and what you like to do—not on what your neighbors' kitchens look like.

Here, for instance, are three examples of very different kitchens, all using the same 12-by-12-foot corner of a room. In the first, the layout is as conventional as it gets, with the sink on one side beneath a window, the stove and oven on another side, and a trim and efficient arrangement of all the cabinets.

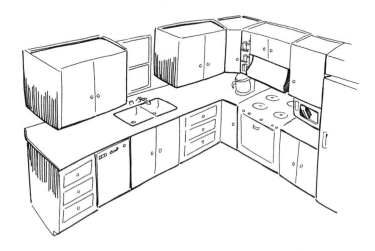

Taking the same essential layout, it's possible to reconfigure things slightly by placing the sink in the corner of the room. The result is a far more compact working area, especially the counter space between the sink and the stove.

Finally, what is essentially the same space can be converted into a workhorse kitchen by the addition of a triangular-shaped island in the center. This not only has space for a pair of seats, it also holds the kitchen sink—which frees up massive amounts of counter space along the wall.

A Budget by Design

One of the things that scares people about kitchen renovations is the cost. There's a perception that a makeover will automatically add up to tens of thousands of dollars, and this alone forces people to accept the grim realities of their own kitchens and leave things alone. In all cases, I think it's best to approach a kitchen renovation from the opposite way. Instead of making the changes you dream of and hoping they don't become too expensive, I think it's more important to come up with a budget you can live with, and make the changes you can afford.

While a gut renovation of a kitchen will always cost a great deal of money, it's possible to update things with some clever thinking and give everything a fresher look for about $1,000. What would this give you? I'll describe all these techniques in the coming chapters, but here's a quick rundown. You could install a new laminate countertop, which, assuming you have an average countertop of about 20 feet total, means you would be paying about $400. You could clean the kitchen cabinets, or else paint them, which would cost you another $50. Changing the hardware on the cabinet doors is also a good way to make a change in looks, and that might cost you $125. Adding a new stainless-steel sink might cost you an additional $125, along with a $100 faucet for the same amount, and another $100 for the plumbing hardware needed to put it all together. To brighten things up, you can add some halogen lighting under the cabinets for an accent, which might cost $100. I'll show you what you need to know to tackle these projects in the coming chapters. Do this work over a couple of weekends, or even one weekend if you have plenty of help, and you'll have spent $1,000. The results may not win you a spot on the cover of *House Beautiful,* but your house will be beautiful in your eyes,

Get a Focus

Designing a kitchen can be a daunting task—just ask the many people who have tried, and not been overly happy with the results. The best way to avoid this, I've found, is by starting out and focusing on a major aspect or two of your kitchen that you know you want to have. Do you crave a giant six-burner Viking stove? How about a double-wide Sub-Zero refrigerator/freezer? Has a walk-in pantry been something you've most wanted to install? Far from being afterthoughts, these major items require planning from the very beginning, and will shape the entire direction of the kitchen design. Make sure you have these firmly in place, and the rest of the design will follow from that.

because you will have radically changed the look of a room that you had thoroughly given up on.

If you've got a larger budget, you could jump up to a $5,000 remodel. This would include all the same projects from the $1,000 renovation, but it would also allow you to radically transform the look of your cabinets. For $3,000, you could afford to reface the kitchen cabinets with new doors—as I'll discuss in Chapter 2—or else replace the cabinets entirely, depending on the size of the kitchen. With the remaining $1,000, as we'll see, you would most likely have enough money to add a new floor, whether it's hardwood, wood laminate, or even vinyl. The amount of time required would be considerably longer, perhaps four or five weekends, but it is still a manageable project that does not necessarily involve ripping the kitchen apart and starting over.

Where do I draw the line between what you can do yourself, and

The Perfect Floor

Back in those oh-so-stylish 1970s, a friend of mine reports, his Aunt Helen thought she found the perfect flooring for her kitchen: lime-green shag carpeting. It worked well enough and certainly kept her feet warm—that is, until one memorable day when she slid the homemade lasagna out of the oven and upended it on her misguided attempt at décor.

Let's face it, a kitchen floor is one hardworking surface, and people try every combination of materials from hard slate to soft-padded vinyl until they settle, like Goldilocks, on something that's just right. For me, the material that makes the most sense in the kitchen is wood. It's beautiful, which should satisfy those looking for something stylish. It's also easy on the feet, which will satisfy those seeking comfort. But, most important of all, a wood surface is completely renewable. After a decade of being abused, it can be sanded down, refinished, and it will look brand-new. The same could hardly be said for tile, let alone shag carpeting.

You CAD, You!

Take a trip to a computer store, and you'll see row after row of what at first glance looks like easy-to-use design software called computer assisted design, or CAD for short. While the packaging on this software certainly makes it seem user-friendly, the reality is much different. There are two problems, really. First, unless you're under twelve years old, computer software requires a great deal of time to become familiar with and to use with any finesse. Second, even if you can learn how to use the software easily, the software isn't going to teach you to think like a designer. This is something that takes skill, talent, and trial-and-error experience—preferably on someone's kitchen other than yours. This is why designers are paid the money they are, because they can save you time and save you money. While the CAD programs seem catchy and may make you think you're solving problems instead of creating mistakes, I would avoid them entirely. In the hands of a professional, they can be a great design tool. But in the hands of the average homeowner, they can become just another way of making a mistake and dragging along the process.

what you should contract someone to do? At about $5,000. Beyond this, I believe it's always better to consider hiring someone else to do the job. I know, we all watch TV shows and read magazines about miracle makeovers performed by the homeowners themselves and indeed it can be a miracle—if the project is concise and quick. Start talking about new kitchen cabinets and Corian countertops, however, or rearranging the kitchen so that the sink is over there by the window instead of against the wall, and we're talking major work involving carpenters, plumbers, and electricians. It's not that you couldn't do it yourself, but it would become a full-time job. If you already have a full-time job, then it means you're going to be doing this on nights and weekends, which could stretch a major project like a kitchen into an agonizing and

A Field Guide to Kitchen Layouts

Mention a kitchen layout to a designer, and you instantly get bombarded with odd-sounding names. There's the G, the U, the L, and even the Double L, all of which sound more like the neighboring ranches on *Bonanza* than plans for a kitchen. Here's a quick guide to the basic layouts, minus the lariats:

The Galley Kitchen

For this classic layout to work, the two sides of the galley should be separated by at least 5 feet of space, in order to give the chef enough room to maneuver.

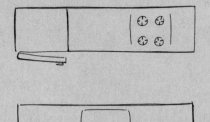

The L By confining the layout neatly to one corner, the L configuration can work well in a great room. It can concentrate the work area in a large kitchen, and free up other space for dining.

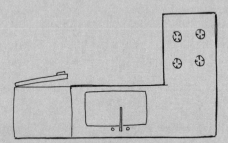

The Double L This complicated layout improves on the single L by
creating two work triangles within one
kitchen. It's ideal for a two-chef family.

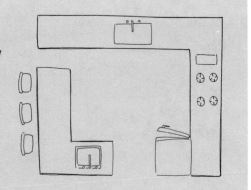

The U By filling three walls with cabinets and counter space, the U envelops a
person working in the center of it and
puts everything within easy reach.

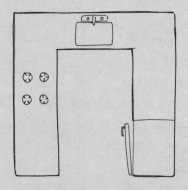

The G This layout is a variant on
the U design, with the addition of a
peninsula that can allow household
chefs to socialize as they cook—and
can also be used for informal dining.

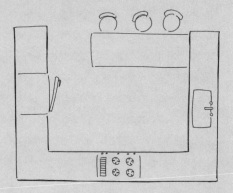

A Design for Everyone

One of the hottest new trends in kitchen design has little to do with fashion and a lot to do with function. It's called universal design, and involves building kitchens that can be used by everyone. The emphasis here is on the word "everyone." The goal isn't just to make kitchens that can be used by someone in a wheelchair, or someone who is elderly. The goal is to design kitchens that are easier to use for every member of a family, period.

Universal design doesn't just mean lowering the countertop to wheelchair height, or reducing the size and scale of everything. Instead, it involves a range of changes that might include lowering one portion of a countertop, and raising another so that a taller person can also find a comfortable workspace. It involves adequate lighting and counter space, so that working in the kitchen can be accomplished safely. It also involves a kitchen that's designed more compactly, so there is less time spent bending, walking, lifting, and cleaning, which allows more time to enjoy the rest of life.

One good example of a feature of a universal design is a knee space right under a sink or stove to make those areas accessible to someone in a wheelchair. That same space also allows someone to sit on a stool in the same location, to avoid fatigue. For these, and a multitude of other suggestions for how to build a friendly kitchen, visit the National Kitchen and Bath Association Web site at www.nkba.com.

chaotic six-month time frame. Even then, you'll still need to hire some-one for the plumbing and electrical work.

Being Flexible

No matter what your plans might include as you begin a kitchen reno-vation, I believe that the most important thing is to remain open to changes. As a builder, I usually try to get people to make as many deci-sions as possible before a project begins. That streamlines the process for me and saves money for them, every time. The one exception to this, however, is in the kitchen. That's because people are far more passionate about this than any other room in the house. In this, it resembles the fussiness people feel for old family recipes, like my grandmother's marinara. You have to get it perfect, or it's just not sauce. Few people feel this way about the dining room, for instance, or a bedroom.

As a result, the kitchen tends to remain a work in progress from the moment the first demolition saw is brought in until the last bit of grout is pressed into the backsplash. Through the years, I can count on one hand the number of clients who have actually stuck to the plan when it comes to the kitchen. Part of this results from being able to see things more clearly as the construction proceeds. Suddenly, the cabi-nets are installed and you realize you should have gone with the big-ger exhaust hood. Or maybe you wish a door to a pantry closet swung the other way.

Little details, such as changing the swing of a door, can be handled with ease. But I'd also encourage you to change the larger details if they're going to suit you better. You might pay a restocking fee to return a major item, and may have to pay your contractor for some additional framing work. The point is, you'll get what you want instead of regretting what you have. As the centerpiece of a house, this is the last place where you want to hesitate because something is going to cost a few extra dollars.

With a workable kitchen—and by that, I mean a kitchen that works for you—you're going to be much happier living in your home, regardless of conditions in other rooms. In the end, you're going to sit back and say, "Hey, I made the right decision to enlarge the space for more storage, or to wait for the type of finish on the dishwasher I really wanted." Now, take out the tape measure and get ready for specific projects regarding the cabinets.

chapter TWO

Cabinet Fever!

Storage, more than any other element, defines the kitchen; all good design plans begin here.

I have a friend named Sally who lived all her life in the old family home going back a century or more. The house had great charm, and what added to it was the kitchen, filled as it was with freestanding cupboards and the sorts of flecked-paint sideboards prized by antiques dealers. As her own children grew up and moved away, she sold the house and built her own place nearby. "I'm looking forward to it," she said. "Except for the kitchen. They all look alike in new houses. Perfect cabinets, with perfect countertops, and it all ends up looking perfectly boring!"

It didn't end up that way for her, of course. With some ingenuity, she turned the kitchen into a showpiece by building the cabinets right. She had wood from an old walnut tree on her place milled for the new shelves and cabinet doors. And rather than filling the wall with a monotonous row of identical cupboards, she mixed up sizes and styles—and even left room for her old sideboards. The result is a place that has a timeless feel to it, with counters at different levels and an atmosphere that makes it hard to tell where the nineteenth century ends and the twenty-first century begins.

In our quest for a unique, workable kitchen, the cabinets form the single most important element. They provide storage, of course, and a way to hide the chaotic clutter of dishes and utensils, as well as trash and the contents of the ubiquitous "junk drawer." Beyond this, they have to look good, whether your goal is to create the "Wow Kitchen," or simply to have a comfortable place that's easy to keep clean. Cabinets also happen to be the single most expensive item in the kitchen, ranging from $1,000 or so up to $100,000 and even more for custom-made cabinetry built with exotic woods. Understanding cabinets, from material choices to installation techniques, makes a logical place to start discussing an overall kitchen renovation.

Cabinets to Go?

Imagine shopping for a new house, and falling in love with a place just because of the kitchen. There's just one tiny problem, the real estate agent tells you: "Sorry, the kitchen's not included."

Laughable, yes, but this could well become the trend of the future. As Americans, we've gotten used to kitchens with built-in cabinets over the last century. A new trend that began in Europe, however, is to do away with this standard look and instead incorporate moveable furniture into the kitchen, in the same way a living room or bedroom is furnished. Some pieces have countertops set on top of them, others hold the sink, and still more piece together to form an island in the center of the room.

Even without embracing this kitchen-on-the-go look, it's possible to borrow elements of it for smart kitchen design. Already, designers work to create cabinets that have a mix-and-match feel to them, and also incorporate individual pieces—such as hutches and cupboards—into the mix. This seems to me to be a perfect compromise. It's a great way to add individual style to a kitchen without scaring off future home buyers—who will most likely want the kitchen to stay.

Cabinet Cosmetics

So, you've spent $40,000 on new kitchen cabinets, and your five-year-old just whipped up a banana smoothie in the blender without putting the top on. How should you clean up this geyser of glop? As you would fine furniture, which is exactly what good cabinetry is. You would be hard-pressed to find anyone taking a bottle of Windex to wipe off the cherry table in the dining room, but that's exactly what many people use in a misguided attempt to clean the fronts of their cabinets. This is terrible! Not only does a glass cleaner do a spotty job of cleaning wood, it actually destroys the finish over time. A better method by far is the damp cloth, wrung as dry as possible and used to mop up and buff clean any spills as soon as they happen. Follow this up with a perfectly clean, soft dry cloth to remove any remaining water droplets, which could spot and mar the finish.

Quality Cabinets, No Matter What the Cost

The span of prices can make choosing cabinets a bewildering chore for most people. Why are some perfectly great-looking cabinets priced at $5,000 for an entire kitchen, while nearly similar high-end versions of the same cabinets go for $50,000? This becomes especially puzzling when you discover that many cabinet makers install doors and drawer fronts made by the same manufacturer. It's conceivable that those two cabinets at opposite ends of the price spectrum not only look the same, but in some respects are the same. You can save huge amounts of money if you learn to shop correctly, and still end up with top-quality cabinets. Let me explain how to do it.

First, drop your prejudices. In an earlier era, everyone wanted all-wood cabinets, which included not just wood doors and drawer fronts, but plywood interiors, as well. While the wood looked nice outside, the particular material used inside didn't make much of a difference—especially since no one is likely to ever notice the insides of your cabinets,

When Good Is Good Enough

In cabinets, as in everything else, always upgrade when the cost is reasonable, but run away when real money begins ringing up. For example, if a cabinet company is willing to throw in solid-wood interiors for a few hundred dollars, then by all means, go for it. But if you're buying $20,000 worth of cabinets, and it would cost you another $10,000 to upgrade to all-wood boxes, I'd say forget it. It would be better to spend that money on things that make a real difference, like college tuition for your kids.

unless you're dweeby enough to point them out. Imagine the reaction of your friends if you invited them over for a party, then said, "Hey, come here, let me show you the inside of my cabinets."

Instead, I think it's important to shop by quality. Nowadays, you can find sturdy cabinets made of pressed-wood interiors, rather than plywood, that have the same long-lasting stability. Even though these may look cheesy on first glance, there's nothing wrong with a pressed-wood box if it's installed and reinforced the right way. The goal is to have cabinets built with solid bones, and those bones can be achieved in a variety of ways. I won't try to argue that a pressed-wood box is stronger than a plywood box. It's not. But once the cabinet is assembled and attached securely to the wall, you won't know the difference. Either will give you adequate strength. And pressed-wood interiors will give you strength with a big savings.

Kitchen Hardware

One place where upgrades are worth the cost is in respect to hardware. By this, I'm referring to the knobs and pulls that have to withstand a lot of abuse. I'm also talking about the hinges that allow the doors to open and close, and the gliders that allow drawers to slide in and out. Cut back here to save a few bucks, and you're going to end up with a kitchen that annoys you because these basic elements won't work properly. Cheap hardware simply cannot stand up to the daily use that a kitchen is subjected to.

What should you look for? Here, shopping by brand makes a great deal of sense. Look for Amerock, Baldwin, Becker, and Liberty Hardware for knobs and

Goof-proof Drilling

It happens all the time: A homeowner drills a hole on a cabinet door for a new knob, only to discover that he's drilled the hole on the wrong side of the door. Believe me, I've done it myself. To avoid this, always open the cabinet first before marking the hole to drill. With the door open, this is one mistake that's impossible to make.

pulls. For hinges and drawer slides, search for brands such as Blum, Hettich, and Grass. It always surprises me that people agonize over the style and finish and type of wood when it comes to cabinets, yet they gloss over the hardware—which is the one element of cabinetry that actually does matter. Even without knowing the brand names, you can shop for quality by developing a feel for how things should work. Look at a display of high-end cabinets, work the doors and drawers repeatedly, and familiarize yourself with what the hardware feels like in use. Then repeat this

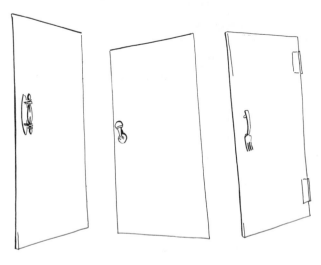

A Better Fastener

Many times, our cabinets come with their own screws. I've never found a cabinet company that gives you a good screw, regardless of the brand of cabinet. Instead, I buy good wood "panhead" screws with a Phillips head or square drive, which you can screw in until they're perfectly flush with the back of the cabinet.

with cabinets that are more in your price range until you find the best hardware. Believe me, you won't be able to ignore the differences.

When choosing knobs and pulls, you can focus purely on the decorative aspects—which is important because exterior hardware can radically change the look of a cabinet surface. Keep this in mind and make sure you select carefully, rather than reaching for whatever knobs happen to be tossed in the sale bin at the local home center. To widen your search, turn to the Internet, where countless Web sites offer entire catalogs of hardware to choose from. Often, you can accomplish a great transformation with new knobs, pulls, hinges, and drawer glides alone—so much that it can form the basis of an entire kitchen makeover.

Installing Cabinets

Some years ago, I was called in to help bail out a "do-it-yourself" kitchen remodel that went strangely awry. The homeowners cleared out the old cabinets, bought the new ones, and began installing an entire wall of base cabinets and wall cabinets. So far, so good. The concept of leveling the cabinets eluded them, however, and so they set about using what they thought were perfect guides: the floor and the ceiling. Surely these were level, they thought.

Not quite. As in most houses, the ceiling and floor existed in two entirely different planes—as the results in this experiment in renovation revealed. Far from being level, the floor dove more than 2 inches from

Anatomy of a Cabinet

Know a kick plate from a lazy Susan? Here's Lou's tour of a complete cabinet system:

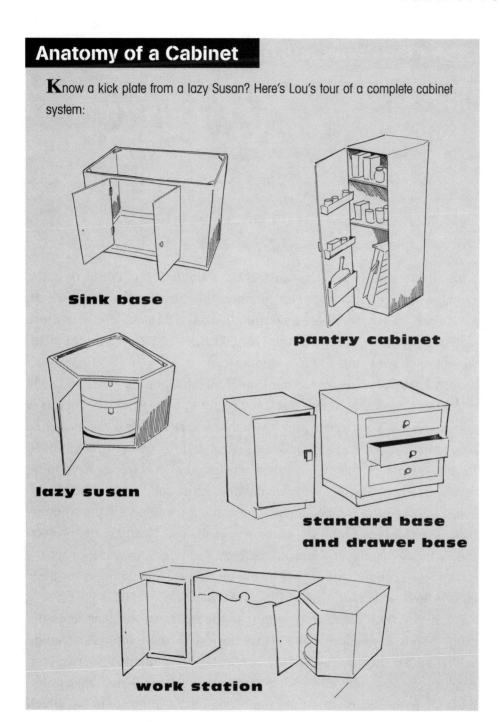

Sink base

pantry cabinet

lazy susan

**standard base
and drawer base**

work station

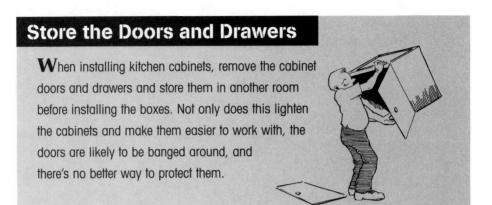

Store the Doors and Drawers

When installing kitchen cabinets, remove the cabinet doors and drawers and store them in another room before installing the boxes. Not only does this lighten the cabinets and make them easier to work with, the doors are likely to be banged around, and there's no better way to protect them.

one end to the other, and the cabinets dove along with it. For its part, the ceiling was living out its own independent linearity, as were the wall cabinets lined up with it. The whole thing looked ridiculous and was more suited to a Fun House than, say, *This Old House.* "Help!" said the man, summing up his complaint in a single word.

As homeowners, we spend our time thinking about the color and style of cabinets, but rarely about how they're going to be installed. Yet this is something that you need to know, whether you're having someone install the cabinets or you're getting out the level and the power drill yourself. Installing cabinets has two primary challenges. First, things have to be firmly attached. Second, and equally important, they have to be level—especially the base cabinets, which form the foundation for the countertops. The real problem lies not so much in the complexity of the project, but in the geometry of a house. Ceilings and floors are rarely parallel, which is as true of new houses as old ones. Installing cabinets requires careful leveling and measuring along the way.

With the room completely empty, a good cabinet installer finds the highest spot on the floor—and, as we have seen, there often is a change in elevation even if it's just a ½ inch or so. Determining this is a two-step process. First, arbitrarily pick a spot on the floor. From this point, measure a line up to where the top of the base cabinets will be, which

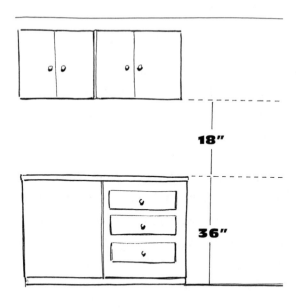

18"

36"

is typically a rise of 34½ inches. From this one point, a level line is then drawn on the wall all around the kitchen, which shows where the top of the base cabinets will be. This line can be drawn tediously with a four-foot level moved around the kitchen, but the margin for error is huge. Instead, I prefer a laser level, which retails for about $70. When the level is positioned at this one point, it will beam a red line all the way around the kitchen, which can then be traced by pencil. Now comes the second step. With the line in place, the installer measures all around to find the floor's highest elevation, that is, the point where the distance between the floor and the line is the smallest. It might be 34¼ inches; it might be 34 inches. When the highest spot is found, a new line is measured up 34½ inches and projected onto the wall and penciled. This becomes the reference line for the installation. The goal, then, is to position all the cabinets so they are parallel to this line.

This involves some additional measurements. The first will be the thickness of the countertop-to-be. This usually ranges between 1 and 2 inches, depending on the material. A third line is drawn all around the kitchen to mark the tops of the countertops. Now comes the line for the wall cabinets. Typically, there is an 18-inch space between the tops of the counters and the bottoms of the wall cabinets. This should be measured, then a line drawn around the kitchen that is parallel to the previous three lines. The mistake comes when people line the wall cabinets up with the ceiling, which most likely would not be parallel to the coming countertops. Often, people try to squeeze the tallest wall cabinets they can into a space, and in this case a different system of finding the level installation line has to be used. Here, a good installer will find the lowest point of the ceiling, and measure down from that in order to locate the bottom of the wall cabinets. By using the laser level, you insure that the line will still be parallel to the one first drawn.

Now comes the actual installation. Logic often tells people to install the base cabinets first, but the opposite is true. The wall cabinets have to be positioned first, because it would otherwise be difficult to maneuver them with the base cabinets in the way. This would be a great way to throw out your back, but not the best way to install the wall cabinets. By installing the wall cabinets first, you can get right up underneath them and get really close by. Remember: These things are heavy, especially if you've bolted several of them together. To hold the cabinets during installation, I first screw in a temporary support called a ledger board at the line I've drawn marking the bottom of the wall cabinets. This not only makes it easy to line the cabinets up, it gives you something to rest the cabinets against while attaching them.

Next comes the attachment. Wall cabinets have to be screwed directly into the studs, which are

A Shim with Shimmy

When installing cabinets, many contractors and homeowners reach for whatever is at hand to shim a cabinet, and often end up with a cedar shingle that they cut down to size. But cedar is soft and will compress under the weight of cabinets and countertops over time. A better choice is a plastic composite shim, made specifically for the purpose. It's harder than cedar and won't give, which means no settling will occur.

the pieces of lumber running vertically in the wall, rather than into the drywall. This is crucial because we're not talking about picture frames here. We're talking about something that can weigh 100 pounds or more when fully loaded. To make sure I hit a stud, I always use an electronic "stud finder" that beeps when it is passed over the solid wood. When I locate the studs, I then transpose that location to the back of the cabinet I'm about to hang and predrill the hole in order to be able to install a good, strong wood screw. This keeps things neater, and allows the process to go quickly rather than to leave your helper or spouse in agony holding up the cabinets while you locate the studs. I use two pairs of 3-inch wood screws for each cabinet, and locate them about 3 inches up from the bottom and 2 inches down from the top. This gives you the most stability when the cabinet is installed, and believe me, there's no such thing as attaching a cabinet too securely to the wall. Call me fussy, but I hate the look of these screw heads when I open up cabinets. To cover them up, I find a bottle of nail polish in a color that matches the cabinets, and dab a little on the shiny metal to make them blend in better. This mini-manicure provides just enough camouflage to conceal the screw from all but close-up inspection.

Base cabinets require a slightly different installation technique. Like wall cabinets, they are also attached to the wall with 3-inch wood screws. But, unlike wall cabinets, they rest on the floor, which means you sometimes have a slanted surface to contend with. Base cabinets have to be installed securely because they're going to be carrying not just the weight of what's in the cabinets, but the weight of the countertops, as well. This is the last thing you want to see wiggle or rock. One mistake novices make is to install a line of cabinets starting at one end and working down toward the other. The problem with this is that the sink cabinet requires the most exacting installation, and it often lies in the center of the row. If you're off by an inch or two by the time you reach the center section, it could throw off everything, from the plumbing to the way the sink is aligned beneath a window. Instead, install the sink base first,

Reface or Replace?

When weighing the option of replacing or refacing cabinets, ask this question: Do you like your cabinets and kitchen layout just as they are? If yes, then refacing them will freshen things up. If no, then replacing them will likely be the better option.

then continue with the cabinets on either side of it.

The key to solid construction is called the shim, a slender piece of wood that gets tapped beneath the cabinet to insure that it is touching the floor securely on all edges and that it is level. This has to be done before the cabinets are screwed into place. Depending on the slope of the floor, some of the shims may end up being doubled up and tripled up until they're quite thick—½ inch or more. While stacking up shims for small gaps works well, this becomes a problem when the gap expands beyond ½ inch because the shims can slip. For greater stability, I would recommend using scraps of hardwood flooring such as oak or maple, which can be cut by a professional with a table saw to the size needed. Since the shims will be visible from the front, this area needs to be covered with base trim to conceal it.

As for the fate of the Fun House kitchen I described earlier, the fix was fairly straightforward. We removed the cabinets and started over, making sure we drew a level line to guide us, and with plenty of heavy-duty shims to compensate for that sloping floor. "That looked so easy I could do it myself," joked the homeowner. And who knows? Maybe next time he will.

A New Face for Old Cabinets

To remake a kitchen, you don't always need to add new cabinets. Sometimes you can freshen up the existing ones through a process called refacing. This involves adding new doors as well as a veneer in some cases to cover the cabinet frames. How do you decide whether to replace or reface? That depends on whether you like your cabinets and your

My Favorite Cabinet Finishes

Let me confess a preference right here: I love kitchen cabinets finished in natural wood. Don't let my taste influence yours, however, especially since there is a range of possibilities and prices.

Thermal Foil Depending on your budget, there's no need to spend a fortune on what will be long-lasting cabinets. Filling this niche are kitchen cabinets faced in a thick plastic coating called thermal foil. The doors and cabinet fronts are made of medium density fiberboard, or MDF, then coated with the thermal foil that is "heat shrunk" in place. The result is a surface that's durable, easy to keep clean, and very inexpensive.

Painted Cabinets High-quality painted cabinets aren't actually "painted." Instead, the deep lustrous finish that tops them comes from layer upon layer of lacquer, which forms a durable finish similar to that found on automobiles. Ordinary painted cabinets can chip easily, and the brush strokes are impossible to conceal. Lacquer surfaces are perfectly smooth and resistant to chipping. On cabinets of this quality, the doors are often made of MDF, rather than solid wood. MDF expands and contracts less than ordinary wood, which prevents cracking in the finish near joints.

Wood Cabinets What I love about wood cabinets is the variety of woods and finishes you can choose, from maple and oak to burled walnut. No matter what look you're after, there's a wood that can complement it, whether you leave it natural, or choose it stained. Well-made cabinets are coated with multiple layers of polyurethane or waterborne finishes that have been cured with heat, rather than just brushed on until they dry. This gives them an extra-tough finish that helps them hold up to day-to-day abuse as well as moisture foisted on them in the kitchen.

A Face-Off

Kitchen cabinets come in countless styles, but no matter what they look like all of them fit into two standard categories. They're either built with face-frame construction or box (frameless) construction. What's the difference? A face-frame cabinet, as its name suggests, literally has a frame that forms a rim around the front of the cabinet. Not only does this hide the way the cabinet is held together, it also provides an easy location to attach hinges. In addition, the frame adds a great deal of strength to the cabinet box. A frameless cabinet, again as its name suggests, has no frame at all. Instead, it is held together by a solid top and back panel that are sometimes absent in face-frame cabinets. In addition to losing the frame, these cabinets also lose an easy place to attach a hinge. Instead, they rely on "hidden hinges" that attach on the side of the cabinet box. As to which one is better, that depends on the look you're after. The frameless cabinets have a more European or contemporary appeal. Face-frame cabinets are built in a more traditional American way, and are often more expensive. If you buy quality cabinets, however, either type will be strong and durable enough to withstand kitchen life.

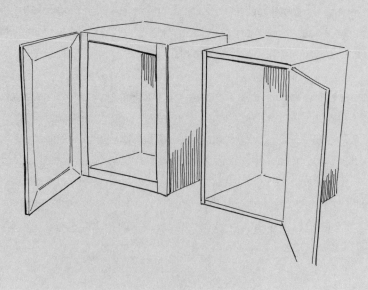

kitchen layout. If you don't, replace them. If you do, you can consider refacing them.

My wife's Aunt Mary and her Uncle Jack confronted this choice themselves. In a world of giant kitchens, they have one of the tiniest. It's literally about 8 feet of running cabinets, shaped into an L. With their children grown, they had no real desire to do a full kitchen renovation, but they did want to freshen up the way things looked, and so they opted to reface the cabinets. Uncle Jack did it himself. He ordered new doors and bought new hinges. He removed the old doors, then sanded down and painted the cabinet frames. With the new doors on, the cabinets looked fantastic, like they were brand-new. A refacing job such as this, especially if you do the job yourself, might cost a maximum of about $500 to $700. Refacing generally costs about 20 to 30 percent less than new cabinets, so there is certainly a good argument to be made for saving money.

Where the cost consideration becomes more difficult is where you have a larger kitchen. Here, you have to closely examine how the cabinets are holding up. Are all the drawers working properly? Is the layout exactly what you want? Sometimes refacing can cost only marginally less than replacing the kitchen cabinets. Of course, replacing the cabinets entirely also entails other costs and more time, because you end up having to take off the countertop and disconnect and reinstall the sink. But you do have to ask yourself, if you're going to reface for $3,500, but can replace for $4,500, is that thousand dollars saved worth it? Replacing the cabinets outright also allows you the possibility of augmenting them with things you've always wanted, such as interior slide-outs in base cabinets to hold heavy pots and small appliances. Perhaps you've always wanted to move the kitchen sink over a foot, so that it is centered beneath a window? Replacing the kitchen cabinets also offers you the opportunity to do that, in a way that refacing simply does not.

Once you've decided to reface cabinets, you have to search for new doors and hardware. These are available over the Internet and by catalog through the mail, in addition to home improvement centers. In many

All Dressed Up

Once you've sorted out what kind of cabinets you want and what the layout should be, you're only partly done. There is still the issue of how to dress them up—with crown molding, spacers to hide gaps, and an assortment of other trim that can add architectural distinction to an otherwise humdrum kitchen. The search can even allow for some creative liberties.

A perfect example can be found in my own kitchen, where we have a large two-tiered island that houses the sink and dishwasher. When we remodeled recently, I added the island and envisioned it to be everything from an eating area to a place where my four kids could do their homework. I knew I needed support legs to hold it up, but wasn't sure what type. The 2-by-4s I put in as supports were temporary, to be sure.

At first, I thought of adding turned legs, like on a piano, made of the same wood as the cabinets. We have stainless-steel appliances, however, and my wife, Mary Beth, suggested something else one day: "Why can't we just add stainless-steel legs?" That sounded intriguing to me. I found a supplier who sold me a pair of 6-inch-diameter stainless-steel pipes, and fabricated legs out of them. Two weeks later, the job was done. The new legs not only hold up the island but totally tie it in to the rest of the kitchen. It marks the perfect balance between design and spontaneity.

cases, the manufacturers of various types of cabinets use the same small collection of door manufacturers. In addition to making things look new, the style can also be radically changed because you're adding the doors and drawer panels over the flat plain boxes that remain in your kitchen—which have no inherent style of their own. Your cabinets might date back to the 1940s and look like they survived the Battle of the Bulge, but if the frames are solid you should be able to make a remarkable transformation.

Replacing the doors is a straightforward task, but refinishing the cabinet frames requires additional care. One method is to sand and paint or

stain the finish, which is the most straightforward. Another more difficult approach for the frames is to add a wood veneer on top of the old
beat-up wood. The veneer contains contact glue on one side that adheres
to the cabinet frame when touched with a hot tool similar to an iron.
When the veneer is firmly in place, you then trim the edges with a sharp
knife to produce a brand-new wood front for the cabinet. Done well, the
veneer looks as good as a brand-new cabinet.

While expert installers routinely get these results, novices suddenly
find themselves with a mess on their hands. Veneer seems like it should
be easy to apply—which is why it's for sale in so many do-it-yourself catalogs—but it can ripple very easily and end up looking like refuse from a
high-school shop class. Applying the veneer to the cabinet front can be a
particular challenge where a joint is involved, which is where one section
of veneer abuts another. The mistake is to butt the two together at 90-
degree angles. When finished, this looks fake, and is a telltale giveaway
that the front is a veneer. Instead, the pieces should be mitered, that is,
carefully cut at perfect 45-degree angles that lock together to form a
better-looking joint. When it's installed, raw-wood veneer can be stained
and finished just like wood. The result will be a professional-looking set of
cabinets.

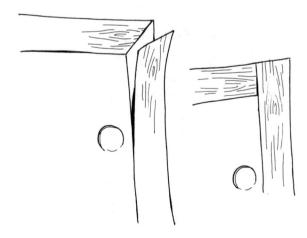

Surviving Trash and Clutter

If the Martians' only exposure to the kitchen of an earthling was a picture spotted in a house magazine, the poor aliens would justifiably be confused about its purpose. Perhaps the kitchen exists as a lavish flower-arranging area, they would wonder, where the occasional bud could be left dangling artfully off the countertops? Or better yet, maybe the kitchen exists as a gigantic visual backdrop to a "dinner" consisting of a single glass of wine and a plate of chopped fresh figs? Wrong, both times. In reality, a kitchen becomes the biggest mess maker in the whole house, and we all know it. Show me someone who roasts a turkey mess-free, or delicately manages the trash after having a house full of weekend guests, and I'll show you a real alien.

Good cabinet design can help tame this. The trick is to make sure you design cabinets for a specific purpose, rather than adopting an "If I build it, I hope it all fits" approach. That only tends to compound problems.

To resolve this, let's begin with the trash. Life has evolved in dozens of ways in the last half century, and nowhere is this change more evident than in the trash we generate. Don't believe me? Take a look under your kitchen sink, which, inch per inch, probably contains more items than

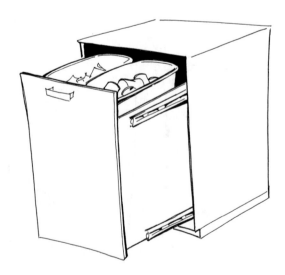

The Designated Clutter Zone

Not even counting the trash, it's amazing to me how much clutter a kitchen seems to attract—or at least, my kitchen attracts. I'm convinced that you could have 30 feet of counter space and an island the size of Bermuda and it would still become a jumble of kids' projects and school papers, bags from the latest shopping blitz, mounds of groceries waiting to be put in the pantry, the latest mound of bills, and stacks of newspaper clippings and magazines you'd love to find time for. After only a day or two, what you thought was a really big kitchen has instead been overcome by all this stuff that takes up the space. The obvious solution would be to get rid of the clutter—which is certainly what happens whenever a kitchen is featured in *House Beautiful*. A more practical, real world solution, however, involves creating a desk area that's situated slightly away from the rest of the kitchen that can serve as a clutter magnet, kind of the way Jupiter absorbs the giant meteors otherwise destined for Earth. Mine has a telephone, a computer, and enough space to hold the bills and the daily clutter. True, the corner does get overloaded, but that's the point: The *corner* gets overloaded, not the entire kitchen. As a designated clutter zone, it keeps the main portion of the kitchen free for preparing meals, eating dinner, and organizing food supplies and kitchen utensils. After all, nothing is worse than first having to clear out a spot in the kitchen in order to be able to cook dinner.

any other part of your house. You simply can't fit anything else. The era of the single garbage can beneath the sink is long gone, especially in light of the things that people keep under the sink, including plumbing, water filters, the garbage disposal motor, and special cleaning supplies for every surface in the house. Not only is more trash produced, but we also have to sort it all into paper, cans, bottles, and refuse for the compost heap. In a large family—take mine, for instance, with four kids—it's a part-time job just managing the trash.

You literally have to design trash into your kitchen, just like the refrigerator and the sink, rather than hoping it can disappear on its own. True, you never see pictures of this in the magazines, which is probably why it's so neglected in real life. Wouldn't it be great to see a spread in *Architectural Digest* on, say, Elton John's ingenious yet stylish trash and recycling center? Until that happens, we're on our own. The solution, I have found, lies in roll-out garbage cans. These fit into an 18-inch-wide base cabinet with a door that is on a roller glide that slides open like a giant file-cabinet drawer. When it's open, standard-sized plastic garbage cans pop in place. Notice I said "cans" because that's what I think you need: two, in fact—one for the recyclable cans and bottles, and one for garbage. If you've got paper trash that can be recycled, it's usually easier

Suitable for Framing

Sometimes the only thing wrong with old wood cabinets is their finish: After a decade or two of service, they have become dingy, lifeless, and have lost all traces of youth. Instead of just tossing out the old, however, it's possible in some cases to rejuvenate the finish. For this, I rely on the secret formula used by antiques dealers who bring out the best in old wood furniture without stripping it. This involves giving cabinets the equivalent of a "skin peel" using what is called a wood amalgamate, which is a concoction of chemicals in a mineral spirit base. One such brand is Howard Restor-A-Finish. To use it, rub it on finished wood with ultra-fine steel wool (I use 0000 grade; the finer the better) and be sure to rub with the grain of the wood rather than against it to eliminate small scratches. The amalgamate very delicately removes a tiny fraction of the finish and exposes a brand-new-looking surface that needs no refinishing. Before attempting this on all your cabinets, develop your technique on an out-of-the-way portion first, or, better yet, on a piece of furniture you're not all that attached to—your brother-in-law's living room end table, perhaps? Done right, it works, and can save you a fortune by restoring the luster of wood without the cost of replacing or refacing.

A Pantry Door to Adore

When building a pantry, make sure the door swings out, rather than in, which will provide more storage space. Be careful that the door does not obstruct the kitchen traffic flow. If it does, consider adding a sliding "pocket" door instead, which disappears when open.

to bundle that and take it straight to the garage. I've found that old newspapers and house magazines hog too much space. I don't want to overload my kitchen by storing them there, since I'd rather have that cabinet space devoted to pots and pans and cookie sheets.

Having this sort of organized system is a neat way to teach your children where your garbage cans are, and it's easier for them to use. It is also a lot safer than stowing the garbage under the kitchen sink, right next to caustic cleaning agents and things we wouldn't want ending up in the hands of our children.

In Pantries We Trust

Another source of clutter in the kitchen is stored food, and the source for all of this is obvious. Do you buy in bulk? I sure do. My idea of paradise is a giant cart and a few hours at Costco. Who knows what I'll come home with—although I know it will be big. A dozen gallon-sized jugs of apple juice for 69 cents each? Pile it in. A buy-one-get-one-free sale on Froot Loops? I'll race you to it. As to where all this stuff goes, in my house it goes straight in the pantry.

I am a big proponent of the pantry, which had its origins in the earliest kitchens as a small room to store food, dry herbs, hang the smoked hams, and keep the giant cooking cauldrons and utensils. When the traveling salesman came through selling baking powder, you needed somewhere to put that five-year supply. No surprise, this room vaporized in the twentieth century. After all, who needs a pantry when you can microwave a Smart Ones for dinner or send for takeout? Well, probably you do. Whether or not you're a great cook, a pantry solves a lot of twenty-first-century problems. For one thing, it ranks as very cheap storage space. Good kitchen cabinets cost about $100 to $200 for each foot measured along the wall, not including the countertops. This adds up to a fortune very quickly. A pantry, however, amounts to little more than a walk-in closet. Since it has a door that can be closed, it can be fitted with simple inexpensive shelving, rather than, say, bird's-eye maple. By having a pantry, you don't have to store food in your kitchen cabinets, which frees up space for the things you do need to store there. Especially if you're limited on space, either a pantry or a smaller pantry cabinet will make a difference in how your kitchen operates.

In terms of what the pantry is, there's a great latitude. It can be the classic small room adjoining a kitchen. If you don't have such a room already, don't despair; often one can be carved out of other space, such as an adjacent coat closet or a portion of another room. This is the sort of challenge that a good architect or contractor loves to figure out. In addition to shelving, a pantry can be rigged with roll-out drawers and any number of add-ons that offer storage space. There is one guiding rule: When you walk into a pantry, you want to be able to see everything on the shelves instantly, which is something you can't do in a closed cabinet as you play hide-and-seek with that bottle of A1 steak sauce you remember having bought but can't find. The most recent pantry I built was an L-shaped room, which doubled as a closet for everyday coats. Along one wall, a set of shelves about 4 feet wide and 16 inches deep stretched from floor to ceiling. Along the other wall there were 24-inch-deep shelves that also went up to the ceiling, but these were elevated 3 feet off the ground—which created a big place on the floor to stow heavy recycling containers, the vacuum cleaner, and even a storage box for dog food.

For a pantry to work best, it needs deep shelves. I prefer 24 inches, which is twice the depth of the typical shelf in a wall cabinet. The wider

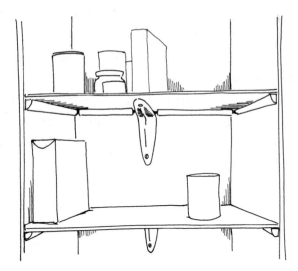

shelves make great practical sense, especially for families because you can store so much on them, from cereal to jars of ketchup and boxes of macaroni and cheese. Second, those shelves have to be strong since they're going to hold a great deal. As far as materials, I'm all for utility. What works really well for shelving is ¾-inch medium density fiberboard, or MDF, which is as inexpensive as it is sturdy.

Furthermore, the shelves will need to be supported with what are called cleats around the perimeter, which are boards about 1 inch thick and 2 inches wide. These provide a solid support for the shelves to rest on. The cleats have to be attached to structural boards in the wall with screws, rather than nails, since nails have a bad habit of prying loose over time. If a shelf has a span of more than 30 inches, it will need to be supported in the center. Here, there are two options. One is to add an angle bracket that is attached with screws to the wall beneath the shelf. The other is a center support cleat, which is literally a post that runs from the floor to the ceiling and helps carry the load. Without either of these, wide shelves will bow and could eventually buckle.

If you don't have space for a separate room, a pantry is still possible in the form of a floor-to-ceiling storage area known as a utility cabinet. For this to make practical food-storage sense, it should be at least 24 inches wide with shelves that are also 24 inches deep, and stand 8 feet tall. Better yet would be a cabinet that is 36 inches wide—about the width of a full-sized refrigerator.

While cabinets are crucial to a good kitchen, they form the support base for something equally important: the countertops. In the next chapter, we'll examine the practical realities—and common misperceptions—of these hardworking surfaces.

chapter THREE

Counter Intelligence

Here's the recipe for creating a hardworking surface that looks great.

First-time experiences often turn out to be the most memorable, and so it was with a countertop project I worked on early in my career.

My partner Mike and I were eager to take any job we could, when along came Marvin, a retired guy with lots of spare time on his hands. He evidently decided to apply this toward the design of a new kitchen, which seemed straightforward enough—until we took a closer look at the plans for the countertops. Working with an architect, Marvin envisioned this as a divider between the kitchen and family room. The main countertop was to be made of solid-surface material, better known as Corian. Installing this required us to get special training and certification from the manufacturer. No problem there. Above this, however, Marvin intended what I can only call a free-form second-story countertop to be used as a shelf, and to be built out of plastic laminate, née Formica. According to the plans, this was to sit on steel columns on top of the main countertop. This was not something you see in the typical home improvement center, to be sure; in fact, from the drawings, it resembled something you'd be more likely to find in the International Space Station.

Mike and I worked in Marvin's garage through the winter, squinting

Highs and Lows

One of the things we often forget to think about when installing a countertop is its height from the floor. Standard dimensions are from 35 to 37 inches tall, depending on the thickness of the countertop. We no longer live in the "standard age," however, so in reality you can make the countertops however high or low you like. My brother-in-law Peter, a giant of a man at 6 foot 2, took this advice to heart when he renovated his family's kitchen, a U-shaped layout with an island in the center. The countertops within the U are a Boy Scout regulation 36 inches high, which pleases Peter's wife and children. As a stay-at-home Dad who runs the household and does the dishes, however, he's the one who spends most of the time at the kitchen sink. Here, he opted to have the countertop raised to a full 42 inches, which is just right for him. To help him create this, I special ordered taller cabinets, which cost only a slight bit extra and yielded extra storage space. While his kids have to climb a small stepladder to reach the faucet at the kitchen sink, no one is complaining—since they're not the ones who have to do the dishes.

as we tried to decipher drawings he had made on notepads and napkins. I was skeptical, to say the least, but when it was done the double-decker countertop worked better than just about anything I've seen in a kitchen since. It had shape, style, and originality. "Cool!" said Mike, once we got everything in place, and I had to agree. While I don't expect everyone to run out and install George Jetson countertops in their homes, the story serves a good point. Countertops can add a great deal to a kitchen, both in functionality and out-and-out pizzazz. They can be built from green-flecked granite, volcanic rock, quartz-filled solid surface, the zippiest plastic laminate—and who could forget good old Vermont maple? You could spend $200 on a 10-foot plastic laminate countertop, or you could spend $8,000 for one made from more exotic materials. With such a diversity of materials and prices, you're sure to find a look that makes your kitchen unique.

Countertops rank as probably the most intensively used surface in the house, unless you count the front steps. I wish there were a simple prescription for a surface that will stand up to the wear and suit everyone, but there's not. Instead, you'll have to work at finding the right material. There's a positive side to this process, however, since choosing a countertop gives you a chance to experiment with color and texture and style. Selecting the material is only the first step in building a countertop to last, however. What good is it if it cracks because it's installed wrong? What good is it if spills roll off and splash down the cabinet fronts, rather than staying put long enough for you to wipe them up?

Let's jump right into the fray: How do you weigh the options for a countertop material? This is as difficult a process as picking the right new car. You could end up with granite (the equivalent of, say, a Hummer) or plastic laminate (Did someone say "Daewoo"?). No matter what the material, each has its pros and cons.

The Basic Countertop

Plastic laminate is the workhorse in the stable of kitchen countertops. Amazingly, this material seems to be every bit at home in a modern kitchen as it was when it debuted more than a half century ago.

While various colors and textures move in and out of fashion—the emphasis today, for instance, is on "vegetable" colors such as eggplant and orange—the basic material is similar to what your parents or even

Counter Offensive

Laminate countertops are usually attached to the cabinets with 2½-inch screws that are driven up through the countertop. Pay careful attention to the screw length. If you use a 3-inch screw, for instance, you could end up with the end of the screw protruding from the finished counter surface. Believe me, I've learned this firsthand.

The Spill-proof Countertop

Let's say you're pouring a cup of tea on the countertop, when suddenly you add too much water and it runs over the rim. Does the water a) make a beeline for the edge and spill over the fronts of the cabinets and onto the floor or b) just sit there or pool toward the backsplash? We'd all like "b" to be the reality, and there's a simple way to get it.

A level countertop is not an accident. It results from putting a countertop onto cabinets that are flat and level. If the cabinets pitch forward, then so will any spills once the countertop is set in place. The goal is to change the pitch so that it tilts ever so slightly toward the rear. If you're adding new cabinets, the project is a simple one. You simply install them so that the fronts of the cabinets are slightly higher than the rear, by a miniscule $\frac{1}{16}$ of an inch. That's all it takes to create a slope that will give you half a minute to mop up a spill, rather than having it run all over the floor. If you're replacing a countertop, then you accomplish this in a similar way by gluing down thin bits of wood known as shims to the tops of the cabinets along the front.

One caution: Don't just glue on the shims and then attach the countertop. You need to check that the countertop will be pitched at the angle you want before making the attachment permanent.

grandparents may have had in their kitchens. Laminate counters are formed from layers of kraft paper saturated with a melamine resin and bonded together under pressure. Because anything can be printed on the paper used in these layers, there's no limit to the look of the finished countertop. As a result, manufacturers offer literally hundreds of colors and patterns, as well as sheen levels that range from matte to satin to high gloss. Of all the textures, the matte finish shows scratches the least and is the most durable. The high-gloss finish is the least forgiving surface, since every nick will show. Unfortunately, it's also the finish that looks the most convincing when paired with stone-printed patterns. A good compromise is the middle-of-the-road sheen finish. It provides a decent look, with a fairly durable finish. Regardless, the selections available will boggle your mind—as will the price, which starts as low as $10 per square foot. The beauty of this material is the cost. If you grow tired of it or it begins to appear worn-looking in four or five years, you can afford to simply rip it out and put another countertop in.

Plastic laminate does have its downside. Chief among the complaints is that it's not very durable. It scratches, it stains, and if you inadvertently put a hot pot on it the surface will not only scorch but melt. In addition, it suffers from being ordinary. If you're trying to create a kitchen that packs a punch, keep looking for a more distinctive material. Still, these countertops make a great choice for a budget kitchen or for anyone trying to do a quick makeover. One caution: The maximum counter length for a slab of plastic laminate is 12 feet. While two pieces can be joined together to create a longer stretch, there will be a visible seam at that point.

Would You Like Wood?

One rustic yet good-looking material is butcher's block, which is usually made of a 1½-inch-thick slab of laminated maple and costs anywhere from $50 to $100 per square foot depending on the quality. While I've never installed an entire countertop made of this, it makes a great accent

Don't Make That Cut!

If you look in most books and magazines that compare countertops, they will blithely rate the surfaces according to whether or not you can freely chop on them with knives. Solid surface countertops and wood usually rate high for slicing, while granite, plastic laminate, and concrete rate low. My advice? Except for actual butcher's block, don't make a habit of chopping on a countertop, no matter what the material is. Not only will you dull the knives, but even if you don't destroy the counter surface outright you will put it under great stress and give it a worn look in no time. Instead, use small portable wooden cutting boards for slicing and dicing, or add pull-out cutting boards that slide out just beneath the countertops. You'll help preserve your knives, as well as your countertops.

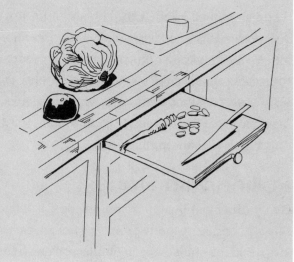

on islands or as chopping block inlays into countertops made of other materials. Beyond the warm look of wood, butcher's block has a great practicality. For one thing, you can slice on it with abandon, which is something you would avoid on just about every other surface. Where plastic laminate and even granite would scratch, butcher's block actually thrives on the abuse. Head to an actual butcher shop and you'll see what I mean. There, you'll find a surface that has so many scratches and nicks that it's nowhere near flat. It's been eroded by knives, much like the Grand Canyon was shaped by the Colorado River, and has great character as a result.

A wood countertop does have its weaknesses, however, as anyone who has ever run a wood chopping block through the dishwasher has discovered. It very quickly starts to dry, warp, and delaminate, and the same will be true of the wood on a countertop if it becomes water-soaked. To prevent this, the wood needs to be cleaned daily with a solution made of a drop or two of dish detergent mixed with a cup of water. Add this to a plastic spray bottle and keep it on the countertop for easy use. After washing it off, rinse the countertop with warm water and towel it dry to get up as much moisture as you can. Once a week, the wood should be lightly rubbed with mineral oil after it has been cleaned and dried. This will keep the surface conditioned and immune to cracking. Yet even with careful cleaning and oiling, a butcher's block countertop makes a poor choice when used around a sink. It simply cannot stand up to the constant dampness without deteriorating. Wood requires a great deal of care to keep it conditioned, but it more than rewards your efforts in looks and practicality.

Rolling with Stone

By far, the most beautiful countertops are made with natural stone, and these continue to be a popular choice, particularly in more expensive kitchens. The choices seem limitless, from veined granite to slate to soapstone. There's even volcanic lava stone from France, which has a unique advantage: You can rest scalding pots right on it, because, after all, it's *lava*. While other materials, including solid surface, try to mimic the look of real stone, nothing matches its variability and good looks. This comes at a cost, of course. Natural stone countertops range in price from $60 to $120 a square foot, on average. Some scarce

Counter Combo

With the vast assortment of materials to choose from, many kitchen designers have begun mixing and matching materials. I've seen kitchens with granite countertops, slate backsplashes, and inlays of butcher's block or stainless steel. The different textures and materials really help make a kitchen unique.

Taken for Granite

Love the look of granite, but aren't in love with the cost? One smart compromise is to build a countertop out of granite tiles, rather than a solid granite slab. While solid granite can cost upwards of $50 per square foot for the material alone, 12-inch granite tiles can be found starting for as little as $5 a piece. These would be applied to a countertop in the same manner as ceramic tiles—complete with a wood substructure to support them. The tiles can also continue up the wall to form a backsplash that connects to the countertop. While a solid granite counter-top might cost $1,500 for a 10-foot section installed, a granite tile countertop might cover the same span for only $500. Yet to anyone walking into the kitchen, the impression will be that they are looking at a solid slab of granite. One tricky part comes in creating the counter edge. Granite tiles are polished on the top sur-face only, not the side, which leaves a rough line very visibly exposed. To create a uniform look, this has to be polished by hand, using different grades of stone polish to match the gloss of the top of the tile.

materials can cost far more. Add to this the price of finishing the edge, which runs from $10 to $50 per running foot.

From a working standpoint, however, natural stone is far from the best choice. That's because most stone is porous. It's as absorbent, in its own way, as a sponge, and this is true of granite, slate, limestone, and other natural materials. Granite, marble, and limestone consist of inter-locking mineral crystals with pores between them—and it's these pores that trap stains. Coating the countertops with a penetrating sealer each year will fill in the tiny gaps, and make the countertops more resistant to spills. Yet even the best of the sealers will not protect against oily mess-es that are left unattended for hours. If, for instance, you drop olive oil or butter onto the counter and leave it overnight, you'll have a permanent darkening of the stone where the oil has been absorbed. In addition, stone countertops are massively heavy—after all, they're solid rock—and

Life on the Edge

To be completed, stone countertops need a finished edge. While this can be a straight 90-degree angle, it's more luxurious—as well as more expensive—to add a curve. Some of the possibilities include:

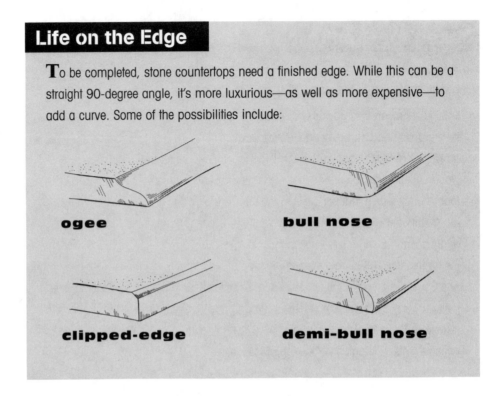

ogee

bull nose

clipped-edge

demi-bull nose

installing them is not at all what I would consider a do-it-yourself option. Troublesome, yes, but the good news is, natural stone will never go out of style, the way that 1950s Formica printed with little boomerangs might. What you put in today, properly cared for, should look just as good a half century from now.

Granite isn't the only piece of stone in the quarry, and two other varieties deserve honorable mention for their good looks and durability. The first is slate. Mention this word, and the image of the black slate tiles used in the entry halls of 1960s bi-levels quickly pops into mind. Trust me, today's slate can look much better. While black is always an option, slate also comes in shades of green, purple, and even a rust-colored red. It's imported from all over the world, some with unique variations in color. For countertops, slate can be cut in large sheets, like granite, that look great. It also comes in different textures, including a natural cleft, which

Stone Faced

Sure, they look rugged, but natural stone countertops are actually the Baby Huey of kitchen materials: tough on the outside, but extremely fragile just beneath the surface. That's because natural stone will greedily soak up anything spilled on it, from red wine and dark balsamic vinegar to oil. A penetrating sealer fills the pores, but it still only buys additional time to clean a spill before the stain sets. Worse, this protective coating dissolves if the counter is cleaned with products containing ammonia or phosphates, which can etch the stone, as well. To guard against this, be sure to wash counters with stone-cleaning products that have a neutral pH (around 7). The inevitable stain or two can be removed or at least lessened with a poultice specially made for stone. Mixed with mineral spirits, it creates a thick paste that is spread on a portion of the countertop, covered with plastic wrap, and left overnight to suck out the stain. Natural stone is a big investment; it makes sense to preserve it.

has a shale-like and slightly rough surface where the stone has been naturally cleaved. Another popular type is acid-washed, which has the smooth appearance and texture of a painted wall. You won't get slate to shine the way granite does, but it's far more resistant to stains. Even so, a penetrating sealer is needed to protect it.

Another popular choice is soapstone, which in many ways is the ideal material. Soapstone has a beautiful look. It's a vein-filled stone, with lots of natural variations and shapes through it. While sturdy, soapstone has a soft surface that scratches easily. Instead of marring the surface, however, these accumulated wear marks give the stone a patina similar to a worn piece of leather. Best of all, soapstone is even less porous than slate. If you spill red wine or oil on it, it just absorbs into the outermost surface of the stone, and wipes away with a little water. You don't need to coat it with a conventional sealer, but it should be wiped with mineral oil once a month, similar to a butcher's block countertop. Beauty comes at a cost,

Renewing a Solid Surface

Durable as solid-surface countertops are, they will in fact become discolored, stained, scorched, or scratched over time. The solution is to sand them down with an electric palm sander, which is something that homeowners are wary of, afraid that they'll ruin their $10,000 countertops.

To begin, I use fine, 200-grit sandpaper. You can tell this by the number written on the back, and also by the fact that it will be a black or red fabric-backed grit. For anyone who has sanded a piece of wood and found it a challenge to "go with the grain," the beauty of sanding a countertop is that there is no grain. You simply have to work the sander around every inch of the countertop, without going in any specific direction. For the corners, you'll need to use an electric detail sander, which has a triangular-shaped pad that can move in tight areas. If you don't have a detail sander, a sanding sponge that has a sharp corner can also help. I then follow up with a few swipes of successively finer grit sandpaper and end up buffing everything with a super-fine Scotch Brite pad. One caveat: The entire countertop will have to be sanded, not just the spots you've targeted; otherwise, they'll stand out from the rest of the surface.

While this is a fairly straightforward task that takes half a day at most, I'd suggest practicing on a scrap piece of countertop first to test out your technique. If you're still squeamish about it, hire someone to do it for you. For about $300, they'll make your counters look brand new—and you won't have to risk ruining them.

however, of at least $120 per square foot. Still, soapstone is such a rock-solid building material that sinks can be made out of it, as well. These are made from cut slabs of the stone that are epoxied together to form an almost indestructible sink—something you sure wouldn't attempt with granite. The look is amazingly built-in and custom.

A Solid Surface

I continue to be a huge fan of solid-surface countertops, sold by brand names such as Corian, Gibraltar, and Avonite. While I like the look of this material, what I really appreciate is its durability. It can withstand just about anything. Better yet, when the surface eventually starts getting dingy and nicked up, you can simply sand it to freshen it up. Try doing that with plastic laminate—or even stainless steel. Solid-surface countertops also have the beauty of being nonporous. They absorb nothing. You could take a piece of raw chicken, lay it on the surface, then wipe it off with a dish cloth, and that's it—there's nothing left on the surface. Plus, solid-surface countertops can literally be welded together to produce a truly invisible seam. As a result, you can have a run longer than 12 feet, or even an entire island, and not detect that it was pieced together. While solid surface in general used to be costly, the price has fallen recently because of competition from manufacturers. You can find decent-quality solid surface for $50 a square foot and up. It is now available with a look called thermal foiling, which adds depth and character to the appearance.

An even bolder option is solid-surface material that contains more than 90 percent real quartz and resins to bind it together. As a material, quartz is diamond-hard. Granite itself contains about 60 percent quartz, so if you have a greater percentage of quartz than this you know the material will be strong and durable. Although equivalent to natural stone, these synthetic blends have a distinct advantage. They're nonporous and do not need to be sealed. They can also be custom ordered in sheets longer than 12 feet and wide enough for an island. As an

A Countertop Face-lift

Leave it to the Italians: In addition to venerable creations such as the radio and the paving block—not to mention a few of my ancestors—they've invented a granite veneer that can turn an old yet structurally sound countertop into a show-piece.

This is possible with a new line of synthetic granite slabs, which are now being imported from Italy. Unlike granite tiles, these are large pieces that look very much like quarry-cut granite when installed, with no grout lines whatsoever. Yet unlike actual granite, installing them does not involve the expense and the mess of demolishing the old countertop. Instead, the new ¼-inch-thick slab is attached to the old countertop with a tenacious epoxy, and finished with an edge that makes it look convincingly real.

The beauty of this technique is that any existing countertop—even plastic laminate and tile—turns into something that looks like granite. The finished price is just over $40 a square foot, which makes this a comparative bargain.

additional benefit, many of the manufacturers that make them offer a ten-year warranty on both labor and materials, which is something you typically would not get with natural stone. Newer versions of solid sur-face match granite in more than just looks. Expect to pay an average of $70 to $120 per square foot, which is identical to the solid stone version. Beyond the extra durability, the solid-surface material offers an advan-tage in terms of color consistency. Because it's an engineered product, what you see on the sample in the store is what you get when it is installed.

One drawback of solid-surface countertops is that you can't rest a hot pot on them. This, too, will scorch. The material is quite versatile in other ways, however. It comes in dozens if not hundreds of colors, and it can be cut and fit together to form inventive designs. You could even build a checkerboard pattern out of alternating light and dark colors of the material. One popular custom feature involves routing a drain board into the countertop next to the sink. There's no question about it, solid surface is expensive—but it also adds value to a home in a way that plastic laminate does not.

Style with Tile

Ceramic tile offers great appeal as a countertop surface, in part because of the comparatively low cost of many tiles. There is also a great versatility in design—from colors to patterns to mosaics. Few other materials allow you this much creativity and individuality, as well as durability. While a cast-iron frying pan dropped onto a countertop or a teapot full of boiling water placed indiscriminately can mar many surfaces, a ceramic countertop will probably be immune to any such damage. One problem with tile countertops, however, can be the uneven surface formed by using handmade or irregular tiles. For this reason, I prefer to use tiles with a consistent surface and glaze, which makes a countertop that is both easier to use and to keep clean. I then use handmade tiles either as the occasional accent tile or as a border within the countertop itself, or, better yet, as a backsplash to form a contrasting surface.

Choosing the tiles is the easy part; using them to form a durable countertop is much harder. In essence, a base has to be created on which to adhere the tiles, and this is often made out of ¾-inch plywood. My preference, however, is for ¾-inch medium density fiberboard, or MDF, because it expands and contracts less than plywood, and therefore offers a more stable countertop base. If you hire

Clean and Light

Dark countertops tend to be popular in kitchens, but keep in mind that the darker the countertop, the more you have to struggle to make it look clean. Everything seems to show. Light colors, by contrast, tend to conceal more in the kitchen, especially if you're a baker accustomed to leaving a trail of flour dust wherever you go.

Keep Out the Grout

If epoxy grout becomes smeared on the surface of a tile while applying it, wipe up the mess quickly with a wet rag wrung dry. Work quickly, however. Once the epoxy sets, it is nearly impossible to remove it from the surface of a tile.

someone to build a tile countertop for you, and to build it the right way, you'll probably spend between $10 and $15 per square foot for the installation. This does not include the cost of the ceramic or stone tile. The smaller the tiles you choose, the higher the installation cost will be. As for the tiles themselves, expect to pay anywhere from $1 to $5 a square foot. Granite, marble, or other stone tiles might range from $5 to about $12 a square foot.

Regardless of the material, the wood base is cut and fitted over the tops of the counters, then screwed into the cabinets. This wood base must be solidly supported underneath. You wouldn't want to span more than two feet without support, or the countertop will crack as it is used. The wood base is then covered with a layer of concrete board called Durarock, which is about ½ inch thick. Now comes the adhesive. While I'm a fan of using a cement product called thinset mortar for a tile floor, the rules for a countertop are different. That's because a countertop is subjected to so much movement over the course of its life, unlike tiles lying flat on the floor. Instead of thinset, which is actually a thin cement, I prefer using a tile mastic for the countertops. This contains no cement, and is more flexible and forgiving when it dries. Instead of cracking and letting go under pressure, it will hold tight and flex ever so slightly.

With the tile in place, it's now time to grout the gaps between them. Again, there's a choice of materials to fill the spaces. The standard grout contains cement, and is completely porous. Not only will it crack, but it will also stain. Countertops take a lot of abuse, with coffee, red wine, and Welch's grape juice spilled all over them. Before long, this porous grout will soak up the stains and look truly ugly. A better solution is to use a nonstaining epoxy grout. Unlike cement-containing grouts, these are nonporous when dry and won't stain at all, no matter what you spill on them. They even come in a huge array of colors to match whatever tiles you're using. Like all epoxies, this special grout contains two ingredients that need to be mixed before applying. Be warned: Applying epoxy grout is a two-person job because it has to be mixed and applied very quickly before it hardens. Regular cement grout may begin to set after forty minutes, but the working window drops to twenty minutes for epoxy grout.

It's a Steel

Another countertop material that has been making the rounds and growing in popularity in recent years is stainless steel. Part of this is purely functional: Stainless steel absorbs nothing, and can be cleaned to antiseptic standards in no time. This is why you find it in the prep areas of restaurants across the country, as well as in hospitals and doctors' offices. The clean look of steel has also found its way into the kitchen, to more stylish effect. At first it began to appear as an accent piece, but now it is possible to have custom-made stainless-steel countertops throughout the kitchen. The look is sleek, modern, and slightly cold, but set against warm wood cabinets it can be used to dramatic effect.

One drawback: Stainless steel, despite its name, is anything but resistant to wear. It scratches and dings easily, from something as simple as a pot sliding over it, and can absorb rust stains. The first few scratches will be especially noticeable and probably drive you to distraction, but over time the surface will become more consistent as the scratches

Dust Is a Must

One way to make a line of siliconized acrylic caulk at the base of a tiled backsplash blend in is to dust it with grout. This gives the caulk the look of the grout, without the fragility.

accumulate, in the same way a stainless-steel sink develops a patina. A custom stainless-steel top can also be very expensive, more expensive even than granite because of the fabrication involved. The steel has to be wrapped over a wood base to give it support throughout, plus the material itself is costly. Regardless, if you're going to use stainless steel, don't try to cut down the price by using lesser-quality materials. Stainless steel is sold in commercial grades of 1/16 and 1/8 inch thick. Always go for the thicker grade; it will resist dings and also have a more substantial sound to it when used. Second, get steel with a higher nickel content rather than a lower one. This is what gives steel its "stainless" character, which is the whole point of installing this countertop in the first place.

Set in Concrete

Believe it or not, concrete countertops are quite possibly the hottest trend in kitchens right now. They're versatile in terms of the colors and textures they can adopt, which make concrete a unique material in being able to express individual tastes. We know concrete from foundations and sidewalks, and while the idea of concrete countertops can at first seem industrial, they can actually be sleek, smooth, warm, and appealing. Done by a master, a concrete countertop can become a dynamic focal point in a kitchen.

Pouring a concrete foundation is the ultimate basic operation. The truck arrives, the concrete is poured, and away everyone goes. A con-

Smoothing Things Out

One of the many challenges in creating a concrete countertop is to create a smooth edge. When poured, the edge has to be framed with a piece of wood so the concrete holds against it. When the concrete is stiff enough to keep its shape but still wet enough to be troweled, the frame is taken off and the exposed edge smoothed into shape.

crete countertop, however, is the essence of a labor-intensive operation. Most concrete countertops are poured in place on top of the cabinets, rather than poured elsewhere and then set in place like a slab of granite. This requires a great deal in terms of creating a plywood structure that can hold all that concrete in place while it sets. Imagine pouring a sidewalk on top of your kitchen cabinets—that is essentially what you would be doing. The actual process, of course, is far more sophisticated. Concrete needs to be finished carefully, in order to make it shine. After it is poured, the concrete is smoothed in place with a trowel, left to set a few minutes, then troweled again, and again. Every time the wet surface is troweled, finer and finer grains of stone within the concrete rise to the surface and fill all the voids. The more you trowel it, the "creamier" the material becomes, and the shinier your countertop will be. Done right, it can reflect almost like glass. Concrete has natural color variations of its own, but artisans also know how to heighten this look with inlays of other stones or even glass beads as well as stains to create marbleized effects. The material offers amazing opportunities, and the person installing a countertop needs to be more of a sculptor than a contractor.

While appealing, concrete has a few drawbacks. First, it is far more porous than granite and needs to be sealed each year, or more depending on use, with a commercial-grade concrete sealer. Second—who would have thought?—it's very expensive, and not because of the materials. You might spend $100 for the few bags of cement needed to mix up the concrete. But the labor involved in reinforcing the cabinets, building the frame, and tooling the material can cost a fortune. This can easily be $200 a square foot, which would translate into a cost of $4,000 for a 10-foot countertop. (Did anyone say "I love Formica"?) Finally, this really does require a skilled worker to do properly. Because concrete is a material contractors are intimately familiar with, many assume they can automatically make a countertop if asked. Maybe they can, but first make sure they've tested out their technique on someone other than you and your kitchen before you give the okay, and take a critical look at the finished product. I consider myself pretty handy, and I can say for certain I would not attempt this without some expert guidance every step of the way. There are too many things that can go wrong, including having wet concrete slop down the fronts of your cabinets, to take any chances.

Backsplashes

The kitchen is the messiest room in the house, of this there can be no doubt. As a result, the more armor you have to protect yourself against mishaps, the better. One great line of defense in this ongoing battle is the backsplash.

The backsplash goes at the back of the countertop where it meets the wall. Grease splatters, soap bubbles fly, spills run—and all of this hits the backsplash instead of the wall. If it's properly designed, you can simply take a sponge to it and clean it completely. The most basic backsplash is a 4-inch-tall rise from the back of the countertop. This is usually made of the same material as the countertop, whether Corian, granite, or plastic laminate. While 4 inches might be sufficient in tidy areas, it doesn't give you the protection I think you need near the sink or by the stove. In these areas, a backsplash that rises to cover the entire distance from countertop to the bottom of the wall cabinets is the way to go. While helping to

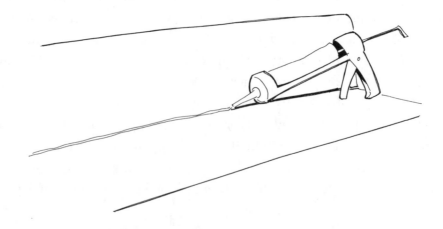

keep a kitchen clean, these also have become great accent pieces, and give you a chance to work in different colors and textures from what you have on the floors and countertops.

Depending on the material used, the price of a backsplash can sometimes be astounding. A full-height backsplash can cost almost as much as a countertop because of all the cuts for the electrical outlets and the shapes that go around cabinets. It gets to be quite complicated to install. If you spend $10,000 on a granite countertop, for instance, you might spend an additional $7,000 or $8,000 to add a backsplash in the same material. And this is for a surface that you look at more than you actually use! In general, tiling is a far cheaper alternative to a solid slab, especially if you shop for basic 4-by-4-inch tiles. Be warned that anything fancier than this can wind up costing a great deal of money. I once built a house where the tiled backsplash contained a complicated rooster motif that had been custom ordered from Spain. The cost for the tiles alone was $15,000, which did not include the cost of having the tile setter painstakingly install it.

In the rush to figure out what goes on the wall, we pay scant attention to the wall itself. In short, how does the backsplash get attached? The typical house has walls made of plaster or drywall, and the backsplash simply gets glued to this with a type of adhesive called tile mastic. This holds firmly, yet is slightly flexible. More difficult than connecting the backsplash to the wall is making a waterproof connection between the backsplash and the countertop. The problem is that with a full-height backsplash of about 18 inches, there will always be a slight separation between the backsplash and the countertop as the two surfaces expand and contract with the seasons. If this joint is filled with grout alone, it will surely crack. While you could simply regrout it each season, this is a losing proposition since the goal should always be to eliminate yearly chores instead of adding to them.

A better solution by far is to run a bead of siliconized acrylic caulk, as opposed to the more common pure silicone caulk you would use in a bathtub shower. The siliconized acrylic caulk can be tooled into place easily without creating a mess. Silicone caulk, however, is very difficult to tool perfectly into the joint. It also comes in very few colors—mainly white—while siliconized acrylic caulk comes in a vast palette. This allows you to pick a color that best matches the countertop and backsplash. Since the caulk is flexible, unlike grout, it won't crack as the backsplash and countertop expand and contract.

chapter FOUR

Pipe Dreams

Here's everything you need to know about plumbing—including the kitchen sink.

When I help people with their kitchen designs, I ask them to imagine their kitchen as an empty room and lay out the floor plan from scratch. I'm always surprised by the outcome. More often than not, they take the existing floor plan—the one they supposedly don't like—and then put everything back in its place, right down to the kitchen sink.

Maybe it's a lack of creativity. Or, more likely, the understandable desire not to increase the budget by one more dollar. Still, in the process of their major renovation, as I frequently point out, the floor will be ripped up, the kitchen walls stripped down to the studs, the cabinets torn out, and even the windows replaced. Sure, it might cost an extra $1,000 or at the most $2,000 to redo the plumbing. During a $50,000 kitchen renovation, however, isn't it worth the effort and the extra dollars to get the sink where you really want it? The goal is to design a kitchen based on how you want to live in it, and if that means moving the kitchen sink and rearranging the plumbing, then go ahead and do it. I compare this to buying a new car, and skipping the power windows in the hopes of saving a few hundred dollars. You might be happy for a month or two, but eventually you're going to regret the choice, when you have to crank down the windows by hand every time you want to stop and say hello to a neighbor.

In your kitchen, I don't think you should ever spend a large amount of money on an improvement and have to compromise the project on something as crucial as the layout, particularly in placement of the sink. Let's review the essential kitchen plumbing elements, to help you make the best choices.

Unsinkable Sinks

If there's one focus to the kitchen, it's the kitchen sink. The sink becomes not only a place to get a drink of water, but to wash food to prepare it for cooking, and to stow dishes for cleanup afterward. Not only is the layout important, so is the material the sink is made of, the workings of the faucet, and the mechanics of the plumbing.

Manufacturers offer sinks in a variety of materials and styles, from gleaming stainless steel and durable porcelain-on-cast-iron to several newer materials. No matter what you buy, this is the one place to make sure you get the highest-quality product, especially considering how intensively you will use the sink. Beyond this, the cost of a top-of-the-line sink compared to a so-so one is not that much higher. While appliances such as stoves and refrigerators vary wildly in price from high end to low end, the cost difference between a good sink and one that won't last more than a few years is often just a few hundred dollars.

Choosing a sink can be a fair challenge given the multitude of possibilities. The first sinks were nothing more than wooden troughs with hand-pumps in them, but things have exploded over the course of the last few decades. Not even considering the materials, there can be under-mounted and over-mounted sinks, sinks that hang on the wall rather than being attached to the countertop, and double and even triple sinks. Lately, the trend has been toward large basin sinks, which have a sort of Depression-era cachet. While the style and materials are important, from

Material Matters

What's a sink made of? Just about every material these days, from the traditional porcelain-coated enamel to stainless steel and even soapstone slabs epoxied together. Here's a quick rundown of the major materials I recommend:

Stainless Steel This is the workhorse of modern kitchen sinks. Not all stainless-steel sinks are created equal, however. Look for ones that are made from at least 18- to 20-gauge steel; the lower the number, the heavier and more durable the steel—and the more solid the sink will sound in use.

Enameled Cast Iron This is probably what your grandmother had in her kitchen, and it still may be there to this day. These sinks contain a thin layer of glass that is fused to a cast-iron surface. These are all but indestructible, but the enamel can chip. In this case, the chips can be covered up with a porcelain enamel kit, which paints on like nail polish. Some manufacturers make a less expensive enameled stainless-steel sink, but the cast iron is stronger and less tinny sounding when in use.

Solid-Surface Sinks While any sink can be installed with a solid-surface countertop, one of the advantages of this material is that it can be paired with a solid-surface sink. It creates a uniform look, but the biggest advantage is the ability to keep things clean. The sink is literally welded seamlessly into place, and there is no visible rim. This makes cleaning up a snap. Plus, as the sink becomes worn with use, it can simply be sanded gently to reveal a fresh, new-looking surface.

One Sink, Two Sinks

More is not always better when it comes to your home. Take mortgages, for instance. One exception to this is having more than one kitchen sink. If you intend to use your kitchen to cook in, rather than just to microwave and wash a few dishes, a second sink for food preparation makes a great deal of sense.

If your home is like mine, the main kitchen sink tends to turn into a repository for dishes waiting to make their way into the dishwasher. When it comes time to prepare food for dinner, the process becomes bogged down by first having to clean out the sink in order to make room to wash vegetables, fill pots, and get the cooking process rolling. Nothing interferes more with a cook's sense of progress! The solution is to have a second sink devoted solely to food preparation, one that is always ready for you to rinse a head of cabbage or fill a large pot with water. An island makes a perfect spot for this, as does a remote area of a countertop near the refrigerator.

When adding second sinks, however, many people make the mistake of installing one that's too tiny, as if it came from the land of Lilliput. My approach is: Go big. While this auxiliary sink does not have to be as voluminous as the main sink, it should be large enough to accommodate a 5-quart pot that's filling with pasta water, as well as a bowl full of salad vegetables that need washing.

a practical consideration, I think the first factor to focus on is the dimensions of the sink.

Some of this is a matter of choice. I personally like a single large sink, rather than a double sink. When I fill up giant pots for boiling pasta or cooking up lobster, a larger sink makes better sense than a pair of smaller ones. Also, it can be difficult to wash a large frying pan in a smaller sink because it simply will not fit. Strange as it may seem, I would encourage you to take along the biggest thing you would ever need to fit in the sink, whether it's a cast-iron frying pan with a long handle or a giant lobsterpot, when you go to shop for it. Showroom lighting can alter

your perceptions of the size of a sink, and testing it out firsthand is the only way to guarantee you're making the right choice. One other dimension to pay attention to is the depth. Choose a sink that's at least 8 or 9 inches deep, although some manufacturers even produce sinks that bottom out at 10 inches. The depth is important because it gives you the ability to wash pots and pans without sloshing soapy water all over.

As for the material, I have to say I am a fan of high-quality stainless-steel sinks. They hold up well, they're easy to clean, they're durable, there's a huge variety, and the cost is reasonable compared to options such as solid-surface sinks and other more exotic materials. Plus, they look great with just about any style, from traditional to contemporary. In my home, I paired a stainless-steel sink

Heavy Metal

What makes stainless steel stainless? It's not the steel; instead, it's the chrome and nickel that are added to it. When buying a sink, look for a minimum of 18 percent chrome and 8 percent nickel. Cheaper sinks have lower amounts of these two metals, but are not as durable.

Mount Up!

As if choosing a material for a sink isn't challenge enough, a kitchen sink can be mounted in two different ways.

A self-rimming or over-mounted sink fits into a hole cut into the countertop, which leaves the lip around the sink visible. This is often the easiest and cheapest to install, especially in the case of a heavy self-rimming cast-iron or plastic-composite sink, which has a lip that rests on the counter and keeps the sink held in place by its own weight. Lighter-weight stainless-steel sinks can also be self-rimming, but they need clips on the underside of the counter to hold them in place.

An under-mounted sink, by contrast, is attached to the underside of the counter. These are more difficult to install, because they require more precision and also a finished edge along the countertop. You couldn't attempt this with plastic laminate, for instance, although it gives a clean look to a slab of granite or solid surface. Under-mounted sinks are also popular because they're sleek looking, and make the chore of wiping off the counters simple.

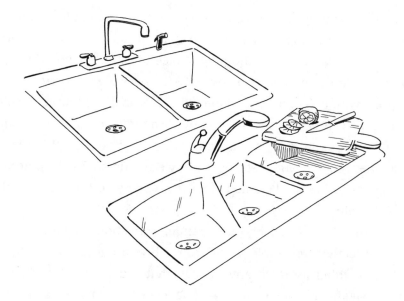

with granite countertops, and have never regretted it—especially during the workouts my kitchen gets at mealtime. Look for heavy-gauge sinks that resist denting, and high chrome and nickel content to resist staining. Plus, so many appliances are stainless steel these days that adding a sink of the same material ties the look together.

Getting a Handle on Faucets

During a kitchen renovation I worked on, the homeowners said they wanted to supply the faucet. This was fine with me, of course, and I arrived to find a beautiful stainless-steel faucet with long handles that retailed for about $700. I gave the faucet to the plumber to install, but he took one look at the faucet and sniffed, "It'll never work. It'll never clear the backsplash." The homeowners protested, and asked the plumber to install it. A few hours—and a couple of hundred dollars later—sure enough, the handles hit against the backsplash and the faucet didn't fit. The couple had to take it back to the store, pay a 20 percent restocking fee, and try again with another faucet.

The number and variety of choices can be truly astounding, and it's important to keep in mind as you shop that not all of them will serve every situation. For decades, the only choice in faucets came down to this: Do you want one handle, or two? That's because the only choices were faucets with a separate hot and cold valve, or those that had a single lever in the center that controlled both. And you could have any finish you wanted, as long as it was chrome. Now, however, there is an almost limitless choice of faucets, both in style and finish. By the time you perused all the options and studied them, it would be time to renovate the kitchen yet again.

Faucets are available in every price range, from about $100 on the low end for a perfectly respectable faucet from a brand-name manufacturer, to $1,000 and higher for decorative faucets that add a note of distinction to a showcase kitchen. Remember: Any faucet can turn the water on; a good faucet is one that after ten years can turn the water off. The key to good faucet construction lies not in the outward finish, but in the construction beneath this flashy coating. Any number of materials can be used in manufacturing a faucet, but brass is the one that holds up best.

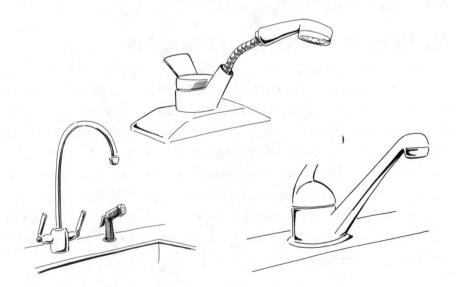

Water Works

Commercial faucets, which tend to have a very high arc to them, are popular in kitchens today. While these make it easy to slide a large pot underneath them for filling, keep in mind that the extra height of the cascading water means it splashes all over the place when it hits the bottom of the sink—an experiment my own kids perform every day in my kitchen. The key is to develop a light touch.

Look for faucets that say "all-brass" construction to make sure that this is what you're getting. As for finishes, chrome remains the most popular, as it has for the last century. It's durable, easy to clean, and versatile. Polished brass finishes have also become popular, especially since modern technology has made it possible to create tarnish-free finishes that stand up to abrasive cleansers. Satin-nickel finishes are another increasingly popular option, in part because of their soft pewter look, which blends in with just about any style.

Another thing to look for is washerless construction. Old faucets contained washers that controlled the flow of water but eventually wore out, causing the faucet to leak. While some faucets continue to be made with washers, the best-quality ones have done away with these in favor of washer-free valves. These can include three types of valves called ball, cartridge, and ceramic disk. While all will function well, ceramic-disk valves are likely to last longest, particularly if your water has high mineral content or sediments that will collect inside the faucet.

With faucets, I believe simpler is definitely better. Of all faucets, the most popular these days are single-handled models with pullout spouts. This eliminates the need to have a separate rinsing spout, which means there's one less gadget that can break. On these faucets, the ones with stainless-steel hoses as opposed to rubber ones tend to kink less and are more durable. One faucet that is becoming increasingly common is called

a pot filler, which has a pivot arm that attaches over the stove. While the idea seems good at first glance—you technically don't have to lift a heavy pot of water from the sink to the stove—in reality I know it would never be used in my household. For one thing, there's no drain beneath the faucet, which to me spells trouble if it's accidentally turned on. And even so, when you're done cooking, you're still going to have to haul the pot back to the sink. So why not just make it a round-trip travel and skip the expense of the extra faucet and plumbing? Plus, a pullout spout tends to rise high above the sink and serves as a great pot filler all on its own, without the need for an extra faucet.

Connections Are Everything

In our rush to think about the sink and the faucet we'll actually be using, we tend to overlook the nuts and bolts of the plumbing behind the scenes. Part of the reason is because it seems too technical—after all, there is an octopus tangle of pipes and hoses beneath the sink. Why not leave well enough alone? Well, for one thing, there's no guarantee that

A Noise to Remember

You're sitting in your newly renovated $50,000 kitchen, when someone turns on a faucet over one of the twin sinks. All of a sudden, an enormous sucking and gurgling sound can be heard, the kind that keeps young teenagers laughing and giggling for hours. What's the problem? Probably the most common kitchen plumbing mistake of all, and one that is easy to avoid.

The plumbing beneath a sink contains a curved piece of pipe called a P-trap, which stays filled with water and is designed to block sewer gases from seeping back into the house. This is the invention that made indoor plumbing a possibility. Now, in order to function properly, each sink has to have its own P-trap, whether it's a double sink or even a triple sink, with a tiny one in the center for washing vegetables. If there is only one P-trap, and the drains from the adjacent sinks simply filter into that one, then a loud gurgling sound will be heard from one sink while the other one is draining. This is because air is literally being sucked through the drain of the other sink in order to allow the water to drain from the first sink. To me, this sound is like nails on a chalkboard, and one that's easy to remedy by spending the extra $100 and having a separate P-trap installed.

the plumber you've hired will do the installations correctly, so by knowing what to look for you can double-check certain aspects and get a solid sense that things are proceeding well. Second, this is an aspect that many homeowners think they can tackle themselves. True, many can, but the "1, 2, 3" aspect of home improvement is often illusory when practiced by real people, especially when tinkering with plumbing. So put on your plumber's apron, and let's get to work.

First off, the sink is the home base for most of the plumbing in your kitchen, which makes the layout and the quality of fixtures crucial during installation. Here you find the main hot and cold water supply, the supply lines to the dishwasher, perhaps the drain connecting to the garbage disposal, maybe a water filtration system, and, oh yes, the connections to the faucet. All of this becomes jammed into the tiny cabinet beneath the sink, which, as I've said, leaves absolutely no room for a pail and brush, let alone the family trash can. There's a lot of stuff going on there, so laying out the plumbing properly and making it not look like a mess is going to help give you a few extra inches of much-needed space.

The way to install all of this, whether you're a professional or a "let me try this just once" sort of adventurer, is to assemble the entire system—sink, faucet, pipes, and all—before you insert it permanently in the counter. This sort of plumbing dry run makes your life easier for a number of reasons. First, you won't have to be crouched under the cabinet trying to make all the connections fit, since you've already sweated through that while standing up. Keep in mind that with a lot of today's sinks, all the hardware, the main faucets, the soap dispenser, the filtered water dispenser, and other paraphernalia get mounted through the countertop. You'll inevitably still be doing some crouching, but all this should be mounted before you put the sink in—which gives you clear access to

everything through the large open hole in the countertop. In other words, the sink hole becomes your friend. Second, working in this way will make you aware of any problems and give you a chance to correct them easily, without having to rip out all your work. You might find that you're a foot short on the connections to the dishwasher, for instance, or that the strainer basket at the base of the sink blocks the pipe coming from the wall. Sometimes the pipe coming out of the wall is set up fairly high; if you choose a deep sink, the pipe may not be in the right spot and the wall will have to be opened up in order to move it. This is especially common in older homes, where sinks were shallow rather than deep. Advance planning will help prevent some unpleasant—and expensive—plumbing surprises. It's so much better to confront all of this before everything is welded and soldered into place.

While the exact layout of the kitchen varies according to the system you have, certain aspects of a plumbing system are constant, and those are the ones you need to look for. The first is the magic connection between the sink and the drainpipe beneath it. These are two different materials: the sink, which can be made of any of a number of materials, and the drainpipe, which is made of brass, plastic, or galvanized steel. How is it they're connected without leaking? This is the most crucial part of the piping system, and it involves a flexible putty that plumbers regard as their trade secret. Plumbers remove the strainer basket at the base of the sink, as well as the finished ring that surrounds it. The putty goes there, between the metal pipe and the drain in the sink. The pressure of the sink resting on the putty forces it to ooze out some, the plumber scrapes away the excess, and then pops the ring back into place. The

'N Sink

When installing a sink, it's easiest to attach the faucets and strainer basket to the sink first, before popping the whole apparatus in place. This is much easier than trying to maneuver while crouched in the cabinet beneath the sink.

Don't Be a Crank

The tendency when turning any kind of plumbing handle, whether a faucet or a shutoff valve, is to crank it tightly in place. The better to keep them from leaking, right? Wrong. Most faucets today and most shutoff valves come with internal washers and compression fittings that don't require the might of Hulk Hogan to tighten. Cranking them hard creates stress at the valves and threads, and that can cause leaks.

result is an invisible seal made of putty that works as effectively as any welding job ever would.

The next crucial connection involves making a seal between the sink and the countertop. Whether it's an under-mount or an over-mount sink, it actually gets caulked into place with an adhesive caulking called Polyseamseal or, in lieu of this, a good-quality pure silicone caulk. This, again, is one of the plumbers' tricks of the trade. Unlike ordinary caulk, this holds the sink in place far better and is flexible, so it won't crack from expansion and contraction. This bead of caulk is crucial to keep water from seeping between the sink and counter, and down into the cabinet and onto the floor below. The seam sealer now comes in a range of colors, so that the finished caulking blends well with the sink and the countertop. You would never know it's there—which is probably why many do-it-yourself homeowners forget this crucial step during an installation of their own.

Any plumbing work of this nature is governed by plumbing codes, but here there are definitely some practices that should be carefully adopted. The first involves the supply lines that connect the hot and cold water pipes to the faucets themselves. For durability, these supply lines should be rigid, which means either chrome-plated brass or a malleable copper. Rigid pipe can be difficult to install, and some codes allow plumbers to cheat and use a flexible hose, which is nowhere near as durable and could burst. Some even allow a flexible plastic hose that looks like a big

Ice Scream

Take a few pieces of ice out of the refrigerator, add them to a cold drink, and what do you get? Often, a foul-tasting brew. Automatic icemakers sound like a convenience, although in reality they are anything but. Whatever goes in your freezer, from the fish you just bought to the leftover lasagna, gives off plenty of odors before it's frozen solid, and all of those odors seem to get absorbed by the ice cubes. The simple solution is to dump the ice bin, at least monthly and perhaps more frequently if the foul-tasting ice is a real problem. With four children in my family, the ice bucket sort of empties itself, but in other homes new ice constantly gets added on top of the old ice, so that you get some fossilized, foul-smelling strata at the bottom that may hold clues to early life forms.

One other way to guarantee fresher-tasting ice is to hook up a water filter at the intake line where water goes toward the refrigerator. You're going to spend the money on a water filtration system for the drinking water, but you won't have to waste money on bags of good-tasting ice when company arrives—and you won't be subjecting yourself to bad-tasting ice all year.

If you entertain a great deal and demand huge quantities of ice, there's an even better approach to great-tasting ice: Install a separate icemaker. These freezers produce between 5 and 10 pounds of ice per day, and are small enough to fit into the space occupied by a single base cabinet, which is from 16 to 18 inches wide. They slide in under the countertop, much like a dishwasher. Since they store no food, they're guaranteed to produce ice the way it's supposed to taste.

drinking straw. Does this sound sturdy to you? No. I would avoid this wherever possible, and go for the more expensive rigid line. For a 20-inch supply line it might cost all of $2 to $3 more to install the rigid tubing compared to the flexible tube, but it's the sort of thing you install once and never have to think about again. The extra pennies are more than worth the peace of mind.

So, What's That You're Drinking?

With care, the plumbing connections in your kitchen will be top quality. Can the same be said for the water that flows through the system?

A great deal has been made of the quality of water in this country in recent years—and, in fact, much of the noise has been made by companies that want to sell you water filtration products to clean it up. The reality is that the public water supply in nearly all cases is perfectly safe and drinkable, which should come as no surprise. The problems, when they appear, are most often the result of dilapidated systems within the home itself, whether it is antique plumbing that leaches harmful metals such as lead, or bacteria that makes its way into the drinking system because of leaky sewage pipes. Finding out whether your water is safe to drink or not requires testing, not guessing. Whenever you move into a home, for instance, you're required to have a water analysis done, which tests for bacteria and other contaminants. If you have a private well, keep in mind that no one is checking the system but you. Be sure to have it tested, and then continue to repeat the tests each year if there are circumstances that warrant it—such as a well that's close to a septic field. Serious contamination requires serious intervention, and cannot be remedied by a mere charcoal filter attached to the end of a faucet.

Yet while most water is safe to drink, the taste often leaves something to be desired, especially for those with chlorinated public water. Tasting more like a swimming pool than a spring in the north woods, it's no surprise that people rush to buy bottled water instead. If what you're looking for is good water to drink, then a home filtration system may be a far cheaper solution than buying bottled water.

These systems come in many forms. Water filtration pitchers are the least technical of them all, but these involve little more than passing water over charcoal in the hope of neutralizing any odors. A slightly better approach involves filters that attach to the end of the faucet. While these are easy to install and more effective, there is a practical downside: they

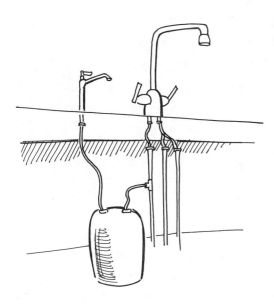

greatly cut the flow of water. Try to fill up a pot, let alone a glass, from one of these systems, and it seems like you'll be at the sink for the better part of a morning. A far better approach, I believe, is to have an under-the-counter water filtration system that taps into the water supply line. This processes water with far more efficiency, through a two-stage system that removes sediment and neutralizes odors effectively. The results are truly tasty; I've been filtering Chicago city water for years, and anyone who tastes it is amazed at the quality. After it is filtered under the sink, the water is then stored in a small tank of a gallon or two in size, and fed through a supply line to a small faucet added to the sink. When you want water to wash up, let it pour from the main faucet. But when you want water to drink or cook with, you turn on the smaller faucet. Chlorine does have its detractors, and for anyone serious about removing it from the entire plumbing system for drinking and bathing there is an even more extensive solution. This involves adding a whole-house filtration system where the water enters the house, filtering water that flows from every faucet—hot and cold, and even the toilet—in the house. The one downside to this, however, is that the filtration system also reduces the water flow slightly, which can be an annoying factor if you're working with a plumbing system that already has low pressure.

These systems are not cheap, especially the whole-house option, which would cost thousands. A better value is the under-the-counter system which might cost between $500 and $1,500 installed. But with spring water going for about $1 a bottle, you do have to ask yourself how long the pay-

Get the Lead Out

The lead content in water, which leaches from lead pipes and lead solder in old plumbing systems, can be quite high, particularly in the morning, after water has sat in the pipes overnight. Rather than installing expensive new plumbing or fancy filtration systems, there's a simple remedy: Simply let the water flow from the tap for thirty seconds in the morning before drinking it. This simple act will reduce the lead content by more than 50 percent.

back period would be, if it means you can free yourself from this purchase in the future. The ease of having the filtration system built in makes it worth the effort of having it installed—especially during a kitchen renovation, when the plumber will be there anyway. These systems have to be maintained by periodically replacing the filters, but the modest cost still makes the water a bargain. As a bonus: It will add to the resale value of your home.

In addition to filtration systems, hot-water dispensers are available. A hot-water dispenser features a mini electric heater with a filter system, and a small holding tank that mounts beneath the sink. If you crave a quick cup of tea or instant oatmeal, you simply turn the valve and 140-degree water comes jetting out. They cost about $250 to buy and install, and are very cheap to operate, which makes them more efficient than turning on the stove to heat up a teapot, or zapping a cup of water in the microwave for a few minutes. Conversely, a cold-water dispenser is available, which chills and filters drinking water. While less practical than the hot-water dispenser, they do have their appeal to some. As should be evident, a lot of these add-ons are designed to make their home in the cabinet beneath the kitchen sink—which is already stuffed full of drains, plumbing connections, and other equipment. If these are an afterthought, they might not be able to fit.

Now that we've tapped the water supply in the kitchen, let's flick the switch to a discussion of lighting.

chapter FIVE

Lighten Up!
With a combination of natural and electric lighting, even an ordinary kitchen can have a bright future.

Sometimes, the best way to remake a kitchen has nothing to do with the countertops, the appliances, or the type of sink. It has to do with the way the light flows in.

A couple of years ago, my family moved into a brick Colonial in Chicago. After moving from place to place over the years we decided this house was the keeper, since we loved everything about it. Everything, that is, except the placement of the kitchen. It faced to the west, toward the setting sun, which meant that mornings in there were as bleak as a city airshaft. I don't know about you, but when I wake up I need a glimpse of sunlight, which does more than any pot of coffee to help me percolate.

My wife Mary Beth and I toyed with the drastic step of relocating the kitchen entirely to the other side of the house so that it would face to the east. Hey, these are the sorts of things you can consider, once you realize how simple it is to change everything about a home. One day, arriving at the place early in the morning to sort out what to do about it, I walked into the adjacent dining room, which is flooded with wonderful morning light. The room has large, old-fashioned French windows that, when open, make the place seem almost like a screened-in porch. The light splashed against the far wall, and I realized that would be the perfect location for the entryway into the kitchen. The light would cascade from the dining room in the mornings, rather than just hitting against the wall.

With a little reconfiguring, I was able to move the doorway and capture the morning sun to go along with my coffee, orange juice, and the *Chicago Tribune*. Luckily, the plan actually gave me a better circular flow in the kitchen, and I was able to add a row of cabinets—in a galley layout—down a 16-foot walkway into the kitchen. In time and materials, moving the doorway and sealing up the old one probably cost me $250, which was a heck of a lot cheaper than moving the kitchen to another part of the house.

Lighting, both electric and natural, is crucial to a home, which is why an effort such as mine is worth it. Here more than in any other aspect of renovation, a little ingenuity goes a long way to create the kitchen environment that you want.

Let the Sun Shine In

Natural light is probably the single most important element that you can add to a kitchen to make it look good. Not only does it make a kitchen feel warmer and more alive, it actually makes it seem larger, which is always welcome. Since this is such a heavily used room, why would anyone want to scramble eggs or boil pasta in a dark, cramped space? With some forethought and well-placed dollars it can become a light and airy showpiece. Look at any glamour shot in a magazine about a kitchen, and the one subtlety you'll notice is all the natural light that comes in. You don't need a kitchen that's going to grace the cover of *Better Homes and Gardens* to get the same effect. The first step in creating this effect is to consider adding larger or additional windows.

Adding more windows is the key to many successful renovations, especially in old houses where kitchens might have had only a single tiny window above the sink. There's no magic formula for adding windows,

The Not-So-Sunny Sunroom

One common solution to bringing light into a kitchen is to bring the outdoors in by adding on a sunroom or an all-seasons room. These have a few drawbacks that I see. Some are modeled along the lines of an English conservatory, and come with extravagant price tags of $100,000 and even $200,000. If your goal is a breakfast room that takes in the morning sun, this can be accomplished far more cheaply by a clever rearrangement of your existing floor plan, and possibly the addition of a bay or bow window to create the feeling of additional space. Cheaper sunrooms do exist, but these suffer from aesthetic anemia. The most common versions might only cost $10,000 or so and do bring in a lot of light, but the look is reminiscent of what you would find at a fast-food restaurant. Instead of building a stylish kitchen, homeowners too often end up with something that would be more at home at Wendy's. Sitting there, you feel as if the late, great Dave Thomas could come walking in at any moment.

Finally, whether English conservatory or fast-food greenhouse, sunrooms are not suited for all climates since they can be very difficult both to heat in the cold winter and cool in a hot summer. To succeed, you need to live in a just-so climate—San Francisco comes to mind—rather than one that goes to extremes. Either that, or be prepared to pay a fortune in heating or cooling bills. Some of this temperature extreme can be modified using heat-mirrored glass. This changes the character of the sunroom, however, since the glass has that reflective look found on the sunglasses of the California highway patrol. While this might suit you, I think there are better options for bringing in the light.

A Window into Windows

The shapes and styles of windows are one thing, but the quality is something even more important. There are countless manufacturers of replacement windows and new construction windows on the marketplace. To sort through them, I recommend shopping for brand names such as Marvin, Pella, Andersen, and Hurd, all of which make great windows. The differences among them are mostly found in nuances. One person may like the way the Marvin window tilts for easy cleaning, and another may like the built-in miniblinds available in Pella windows. Regardless of the details, choosing an established brand will assure that you end up with a great window and add lasting value to your home. Crazy as this may seem, people actually do care what brands of windows are in a home they're planning to buy.

In addition to the quality of the window frame, the quality of the glass is something to consider. Thermal-pane windows, which contain two or three layers of glass separated by an insulating pocket of air, are essential whether you live in a very hot or very cold climate. A further upgrade to low-emissivity or "low-e" glass can also make sense. This contains an unseen film on the outside that allows light to enter but blocks ultraviolet radiation and reduces the heat flow both in and out. Heat mirror glass is a step up from this; it blocks up to 99 percent of ultraviolet light. It almost does too good a job, however, because it also blocks out some of the visible light and can dim the look of a room.

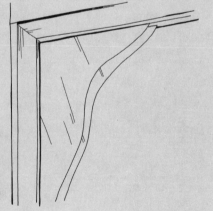

but careful attention to the possibilities will help you create a great space. This is something that good kitchen designers do by instinct. As you flip through magazines with pictures of stunning kitchens, look at them from the perspective of natural lighting and you'll see what I mean. Nine times out of ten, a great-looking kitchen has plenty of light to bring the outdoors in. If you're not lucky enough to be remodeling a kitchen that already has perfectly placed windows, there are several things that can be done. Installing a new window is hardly a drastic project, especially for a good carpenter. The cost of installing a top-quality window and finishing the wall inside and out might range from $700 to $1,200, which, in the scheme of things, is not a huge percentage of a kitchen renovation budget.

The kitchen also offers a great opportunity to think "beyond the rectangle" in terms of windows that can be installed. The typical casement and double-hung windows are fine, but you can bring in more light and actually add more space by installing windows in configurations that jut out from the main room. Bay windows, bow windows, and box windows offer huge opportunities for accomplishing this, at prices that are far lower than the cost of adding an addition.

In my last house, we had a very small kitchen, with not much room for any of us to maneuver. Tighter still was the eat-in area, which contained a single window. We always dreamed of making more out of that space, and making it large enough to be able to create a small desk area with a computer, but simply installing a larger window would not have helped. Instead, I cut open the wall and planned a larger project. This became complicated, since the house was brick. To support the wall, I needed to add a steel lintel across the top of the hole, which cost about $300. Reinforced, however, the wall was ready for the bay window I had in mind.

I built it out of three separate windows, then extended the floor out into the bay as well by a distance of 21 inches. I matched the new hardwood floor to the old, and the result was a new computer area for the kids that added about 20 square feet of living space to the kitchen. This also created much more light in the kitchen, since the angled windows took in light no matter where the sun was positioned. We'd get sun in the

morning as we ate breakfast, at lunch, and again in the early evening, all from this one window. While the entire project probably cost about $4,000, it radically changed the way our kitchen worked—and it did not require a separate foundation that would have cost many thousands of dollars more. Variants on the bay window include the bow window, in which windows are set on a graceful arc, and the box window, which looks like a tiny greenhouse and is usually installed over the kitchen sink.

Even if you can't tinker with the windows—possibly because the wall

Up, Periscope

If your kitchen is located on a first floor and there is no way to add a skylight in it, there is still a clever way to bring in natural daylight. The solution is called a tube skylight, which is like a periscope to the sky. It contains a tube of highly reflective metal that extends from the rooftop in the form of a small dome, down through the walls, and into the ceiling. There it is capped with what looks like an opaque glass lens. Tube skylights have several advantages. First, the tubes can be snaked easily through almost any tangle of walls and closets. Second, the light that shines is very bright and appealing, in a way that no recessed light can be. Also, the tubes can be installed without creating much of a mess, since only a simple hole has to be cut into the ceiling, which is then entirely covered by the lens. Finally, tube skylights are far cheaper than ordinary skylights. They might cost between $600 and $1,000 to have installed—and you'll never have to worry about them overheating the kitchen in the summer, the way you might a skylight.

Subduing the Skylight

While skylights are great for letting in the light, they sometimes let in too much light—particularly if they're set on the south-facing slope of a roof. To avoid overheating problems, look for skylights that contain low-e glass that locks heat, or heat-mirrored glass that reflects up to 99 percent of ultraviolet rays.

---

space is limited, or because it would damage the look of your home from the exterior—there are creative ways to bring in light by adding skylights. Like windows in the rooftop, skylights offer great advantages. Many of them open, so you actually get fresh air through them, and some of them can be controlled automatically with sensors so that they actually close on their own if it rains. One problem with skylights is that many homeowners think they can install them on their own, without any experience. I would caution against this, since I've seen many of them leak as a result of improper installation. Adding a skylight involves cutting through the framing in the roof, and finishing it with drywall, which is a major project. Installing a single skylight in an existing kitchen might cost as much as building an entire bay window, probably between $3,000 and $5,000. It's far cheaper to add these during a major renovation or when building an addition, since they would require minimal additional work and a few 2-by-4s to finish them.

Electrifying Decisions

True, we all want our kitchens to be nice and bright. Sometimes, however, this can get taken to extremes.

I built a house once for a couple enamored with recessed lighting. In the large kitchen, they wanted them everywhere, even though I tried to warn them that there would be so many holes in the ceiling it would look like a piece of Swiss cheese. Even the architect tried to talk them out of it, but there was no stopping them. When the drywall contractor arrived

Lighting by Design

Many times during home renovation we're reluctant to call in the professionals for help—whether it's because we want to save a little money or don't know exactly what help is available. Lighting is one of the areas that homeowners think they can just do themselves, but the chopped-up results usually speak for themselves. Ironically, the problem is that people tend to add too many lights, rather than too few, when they tackle kitchen lighting themselves.

To remedy this, I'm an advocate of the lighting designer. True, people hear the word "designer" and immediately assume it's going to cost them several thousand dollars. This isn't the case, however. In most major lighting centers, professional designers will work with you for free to design your kitchen lighting, as long as you buy the fixtures from them. They'll ask you questions about how you use the kitchen, such as where you eat, where your children do their homework, and whether you read or watch TV while sitting in there late at night. A good designer won't prescribe more lights to accomplish all these tasks. They'll just prescribe more efficient ones, which will create a better-looking kitchen and save you money. When choosing a lighting designer ask for credentials, which can include references from other homeowners as well as membership in organizations such as the International Association of Lighting Designers.

he literally started to moan because of all the cuts he knew he was going to have to make, and the sheets of drywall kept breaking because they had so many holes in them. When the ceiling was finally up, painted and finished, the homeowners arrived—and were horrified at the sight. It looked more like a habitat for prairie dogs than a respectable ceiling. "There are way too many lights!" boomed the man, and although I didn't say "I told you so," I did agree with him. We took down the drywall and removed about ten of them, but I still think we probably could have taken out a dozen others and had even better results.

Adding lights, obviously, requires a great deal of finesse. Take yourself back to your grandmother's kitchen, and imagine the lighting—if that's not too fancy a word. Inevitably, old-time kitchens were not only small, but had one center light fixture in the middle of the room. This was usually a round, fluorescent two-tube light that cast a stark white glow all over the place. While this did brighten up the place, it barely added any character. And it hardly helped anyone see, especially as they were standing over the stove, chopping vegetables, or doing dishes at the sink. They lived their days in murky shadows.

Lighting is important in any part of the home, but it's critical in the kitchen. After all, people spend so much time there, prepping food and tending to the thousand tasks of family life. Having the right lighting not only makes it easier to operate in the kitchen, it also creates a warm atmosphere, as well. Look at it this way: You could spend thousands of dollars trying to find the right handmade tiles for the backsplash, the perfect finish for the cabinets, the exquisite granite countertop. Put in lighting as an afterthought, and this is largely going to go to waste. Instead, spend time and money on good lighting, and you can probably make do with less-expensive material because the illusion will be of a beautiful space, transcending the materials.

Fortunately, we've graduated from the single-fixture days, but many people still are stuck in this mindset, especially if they design or renovate their kitchens themselves. Somehow, perhaps because we grew up in kitchens with simplistic lighting, such as an overhead fixture and maybe a few accent lights underneath the cabinets, we tend to fall back on that when it's time to light our own kitchens. There are two types of lighting to be concerned with in your kitchen: general lighting, which gives everything a glow, and task lighting, which focuses on more specific things. Task overhead lighting is very good as well, lighting over the sink areas, over the countertops. When you're planning your lighting, you want to recognize and keep track of how you think you're going to use your kitchen. If you're a baker, and you love to bake, make sure there will be plenty of light where you work so you can see your scones as you're mixing them. There's a lot to think about.

Some of the most popular lights today are recessed lights, partly because of their streamlined, almost invisible look. Also known as "can" lights because of their shape, they shine from the ceiling, with nothing hanging down to accumulate dust and kitchen grime, just pure light that descends from the ceiling. While the tendency is to just slap recessed lighting around, more is involved in recessed lighting than people think. One drawback of recessed lighting is that it can cast a spotlight, and turn your kitchen into something more suited to a vaudeville stage. A flair for the dramatic can be great in a kitchen, but this can be a bit much. Instead, recessed lighting has to be installed according to a formula provided by the manufacturer, which governs how far apart they should be, and how many are needed to light a specific space.

This formula varies according to the size of the light, the height of the

A Field Guide to the Bulbs

Not so many years ago, a lightbulb meant one thing: that familiar bulbous-shaped piece of glass. Nowadays, lightbulbs have gone wild, with variations from halogen lights to compact fluorescent bulbs that look as if they came out of a Reddi Whip container. Here's a quick tour of the modern variations:

Incandescent Lights These are the bulbs that Thomas Edison invented, and they're all but unchanged to this day. When charged with electricity, the bulbs produce light by simple radiation from a heated tungsten filament, in the same way that a toaster glows red. The lighting efficiency is generally low since most of the energy is released as infrared radiation rather than visible light.

Halogen Lights These are incandescent lights, too, only with a twist. Halogen bulbs have a tungsten filament, but the bulb itself is filled with halogen gas. When an incandescent lamp operates, tungsten from the filament is evaporated into the gas of the bulb and deposited on the glass wall. The bulb "burns out" when enough tungsten has evaporated from the filament so that electricity can no longer be conducted across it. The halogen gas in a halogen lamp carries the evaporated tungsten particles back to the filament and rede-

ceiling, and the type and wattage of the bulb. All manufacturers recommend a formula based on the height of the ceiling and the wattage of the bulb—one manufacturer recommends spacing 75-watt halogen lights every 8 feet, for instance. At this distance, the area is covered with overlapping pools of light, which results in good general lighting. I like mixing up these lights with spotlights to highlight a specific work area, as well as floodlights, which cast a glow over a broader area.

One common mistake I see repeated again and again with can lights seems to defy a formula. Everyone wants to install them so that they shine down on the countertops, but they end up installing them in the posits them. This gives the lamp a longer life, and a cleaner bulb for the light to shine through. Further designations, such as PAR, for "parabolic aluminized reflector," and AR, for "aluminized reflector," are types of halogen lamps that use a precision pressed-glass reflector, which provides more light and lasts longer than standard halogen bulbs. On a halogen lightbulb, the designation of PAR plus a number govern the shape and size of the bulb. For example, PAR38 or AR50 refers to the lamp shape and the bulb expressed in eighths of an inch.

Compact Fluorescent Lamps Say fluorescent lights, and one thing comes to mind: those flicker bulbs that cast a cold, bluish light in grammar school. Not so with the new generation of fluorescents, known as CFLs. These use a different technology than incandescent lightbulbs and provide warm light without the flicker and hum of their infamous predecessors. Instead of a tungsten wire, fluorescent lamps use energy to create an arc of excited mercury vapor across the lamp. Less energy is needed to maintain this arc than to keep an incandescent filament burning. As a result, compact fluorescent lamps are more energy efficient than an incandescent bulb of the same wattage because they use less energy yet provide the same amount of light.

ceiling too close to the wall cabinets. The result is a botched lighting scenario, which no one ever seems to notice until the cabinets are installed near the end of the renovation process, when it's too late to correct things easily. Let's work on a few dimensions for a moment to spare you this trouble. Wall cabinets are about 12 inches deep, and tend to stick out 2 or 3 inches farther with the moldings that are added to them. The diameter of the can light is 6 inches, plus another 2 inches for the decorative trim that fits around it. If you do the math, that means the center of the can light has to lie a bare minimum of 18 inches from the wall in order for the can lights to fit properly. If you're going to use an especially thick

Mix and Match

While recessed lighting has its appeal, more does not mean better. A room filled with these lights resembles the Museum of Modern Art more than a home—and is hardly appealing. A better approach is to rely on a mix of lights, including a hanging fixture or two, to provide both better light and a better look.

piece of crown molding around the cabinets, then you'll be safer with a distance of 20 inches. You will never find these dimensions printed in any lighting manual, believe me. But pay attention to them, and you'll be rewarded with a shower of light on the countertop and a cascade of light on the beautiful cabinet fronts.

Task lighting, or accent lighting, can serve two purposes. First, it provides some extra light when you're trying to accomplish a task. And, second, it looks great to have certain areas of the kitchen highlighted more than others—just so

long as you're not highlighting the clutter zone! The most popular place for this sort of lighting is under the wall cabinets. This floods the countertop in light that makes it easy to work on the surface, and since the light is coming from above your hands, rather than behind your head, it means that there aren't any annoying shadows to be created. The light does not have to be super-high wattage to offer some assistance. Instead, low-wattage bulbs can pad the overall light in the kitchen and create a better work environment.

Many types of lights exist for this purpose, including small halogen lights that have become very popular. These are very bright, and are installed almost like miniature versions of can lights under the cabinets. They look good, since the light is so appealing, and certainly do brighten up the counter space. But the complaint I always get from people is that these halogen lights get very hot, and literally heat up the cabinet space above. While this is not a danger if they're properly installed according to the instructions, they can have an effect on stored food in the cabinets—particularly spices. Your mustard powder and oregano and thyme will end up baking day after day and lose their punch. There are two options: One is to relocate the spices and food to another cabinet away from the light, and the other is to choose a different type of light.

My choice for under the cabinet is fluorescent lighting. Unlike grandma's day, today you've got a choice. You can go with a "cool" bulb that emits light with a long wavelength, and produces that stark whitish glow. Or, you can choose a "warm" bulb that emits light with a shorter wavelength, which more closely resembles

Taming the Heat

To reduce the heat generated by under-the-cabinet lighting, try gluing a half-inch layer of rigid reflective insulation between the cabinet and the fixture. To conceal both the insulation and the light bulb, you'll also need to add a decorative strip of wood called a valance at the bottom of the cabinet.

traditional incandescent light. These bulbs give great general task lighting, and warm up the area that they illuminate. And since they're cool when in use—you can actually touch the bulb with your fingers with the light on—they don't heat up the cabinet space to the same extent. One other benefit of fluorescent bulbs is their cost. They use less energy per 100 watts when in use, and the bulbs literally last three to four years and even more when in use. Try coaxing that lifespan out of an ordinary lightbulb!

Installing Lights

Choosing lights inevitably means installing lights, and this is where most homeowners happily draw the line between what they're willing to consider doing themselves (such as refacing cabinets or installing a new faucet) and what they're more than willing to turn over to a professional. This is a wise move, considering the consequences of doing things wrong when it involves high-voltage wires.

During new construction or a complete gut renovation, wiring and lighting is fairly straightforward. The electrician has free rein to maneuver the wiring everywhere, and the homeowner can make adjustments along the way—like moving an electrical box in the ceiling a few inches, so that it is centered better over a table, for instance. When adding wiring to a room that already has walls, however, the task becomes more of a challenge. The challenge is to keep this an electrical project, and not let it turn into a demolition project. Outlets to hold hanging and wall fixtures are fairly easy for an electrician to install. You might end up with an inch-wide trench cut into the wall where the electrician has to bury the wires to the electric service panel in the basement, but overall it's not a difficult or terribly destructive project. Recessed lighting, however, is another matter, since it involves cutting such a large hole in the wall.

This process can be simplified by using what is known as remodeling can lights. To install these, all that is required is to cut a hole in the wall the exact size of the housing, which is typically about 6 inches in diameter. The new light is pressed into the hole, and clips around the edge of it flip out to hold it firmly in place. With these lights, a good electrician can actually push the wiring through the drywall to make the connection to the switch in the wall. Because installing these lights involves limited damage to the drywall, they can be installed almost anywhere.

Being Baffled

While can lights all look the same, the lining—known as the baffle—that surrounds the bulb can dramatically change the look of the light. These can be white, black, or finished in a reflective trim, each of which adds a radically different character to the same flush-mounted light.

Notice I said "almost" anywhere. Ordinary recessed lights cannot be installed directly against insulation. The danger here is that the insulation would trap the heat emitted by the lights, and could cause a fire hazard. Instead, whenever recessed lights come into contact with insulation—as they would if you install them in a kitchen in a one-story section of a house with an insulated ceiling—a much different unit called an IC light, which stands for "insulated can," has to be used. While the light emitted from this is identical to an ordinary recessed light, the housing that holds the light is different. It is much larger on the back end, with a metal housing that resembles a bread box. This is designed to keep a distance between the light and the insulation, and to provide enough of a gap for it to release heat without creating a fire hazard. All local building codes require these to be used in insulated areas for safety, and every licensed electrician knows how to do this. But for people tackling their own electrical work—and many do—using the wrong lights is a common, and very dangerous, mistake. One way to avoid this in an older house is to test for insulation before buying the lights. To do this, drill a 1-inch hole into the ceiling, which is wide enough for your finger or a narrow flashlight.

One phenomenon that happens with can lights is that they create drafts in cold weather, especially if they're used in ceilings where the space above is unheated. When the lights are in use, the heat generated by the bulbs tends to offset the cold, but when they're off they can create an actual distinct chill in a room. Insulated can lights are especially important in these areas. An additional precaution is to have the electrician carefully use some caulking to seal the gap between the light fixture and the ceiling. A better solution is to look for new draft-proof can lights, which are manufactured by companies such as Juno, Halo, and Contico. These eliminate the problem for good.

Are You a Fan of Fans?

Ceiling fans have long been popular in the kitchen, but installing one that doesn't wobble or cause problems takes some effort.

A Hot Idea

Ceiling fans tend to cool things down—which is great in the summer, but not so good in colder weather. Wouldn't it be novel to have a fan that actually blew hot air into a room when you wanted it?

A company named Reiker has come up with something I think is a nifty solution. It's a fan—the company calls it a "room conditioner"—with a built-in electric heating system inside. You can use the device as an ordinary fan or flick on a thermostat to turn on the heat, as well. Running the fan in cold weather makes the room uniformly warm, with no hot spots or cold spots. Just even, glorious warmth.

The device isn't cheap at about $400, which is easily twice what a top-quality ordinary fan might cost. But it's a great item to consider to add comfort to a room such as a kitchen, where you want things toasty warm when you wake up in the morning. Since it mounts in a regular fan box, it is no more difficult to install than an ordinary fan. It's also fairly inexpensive to run, since it uses no more electricity than an ordinary hair dryer.

The most important first step is to buy a high-quality fan. If you find one for $49 in the bargain bin, you're asking for trouble. Instead, choose fans from quality manufacturers such as Emerson, Casablanca, and Hunter—but even here, choose from the higher-priced fans. It's not the decorative finishes you should be concerned with, but rather the quality of the

A One-Finger Test

A simple test to see if you have a fan-rated electrical box in the ceiling is to try to jiggle the box by poking it with a finger. If it wiggles, you've got problems. If it's solid, you're most likely good to go.

motor and the thickness and durability of the blades. These are the components of a great fan. This is the classic example of "you get what you pay for."

One mistake people make—especially do-it-yourself homeowners, or those hiring cut-rate electricians—is to install a fan into an ordinary electrical box mounted into the ceiling. To work properly and without wobbling, the fan has to be installed into what is called a fan-rated box. This means that the box is actually mounted to structural framing within the ceiling, which is the only way it can hold a whirling fan without wobbling loose. If it's not possible to attach the box directly to the framing, the alternatives are either to install extra framing or to install what is called a fan bracket. This is literally a rod with two pinchers that expands as it screws into place between two pieces of solid framing. The new box can then be safely attached to the bracket.

While it's possible to mount a ceiling fan just about anywhere, a few rules apply. For one thing, make sure it's mounted high enough so that no one runs the risk of hitting it while it's spinning. The classic location for this is over the kitchen table, which keeps it out of everyone's way and provides a breeze while eating. One place a fan should never be located is near the cooking area. While it might seem like a good idea to install it there to help vent cooking odors, the reality is that the ceiling fan will spread grease-filled steam throughout the kitchen. Nothing could be messier. Another thing to keep in mind is the height of the fan from the floor. For safety, building codes require that the blades of the fan be no less than 7 feet from the floor, including when placed over a table. Even though this is the code, I think that's too low—a minimum of 7½ feet is better.

Switching Topics

In the same way that people go wild with recessed lights, they can sometimes go wild with the number of switches they add to their kitchen. Believe me, I know. After all, I'm one of them.

I wanted the light over the kitchen table to be on its own switch, which is a good idea. Then I wanted the can lights in the kitchen and the adjacent family room to be on two separate sets of switches because I don't always need them both on at the same time. Then the lights over the computer area are on their own switch, and on it goes. On one wall, I have a bank of four switches, and even after living in this house for two years I am constantly flicking them one by one to find the switch I want.

Which lights you add in your kitchen is one challenge; how you control them is another. Back in grandma's kitchen, of course, a single light switch controlled the single light. Now, with ten, twenty, and sometimes thirty or more different bulbs, and an assortment of task and accent lights, a more sophisticated switching system is needed. You don't want to confront thirty different switches. And you want to be able to control various banks of light from various parts of the room, especially since kitchens tend to have multiple entryways. You don't want to be stumbling around in the dark in your new $50,000 kitchen, hoping you can find the switch someplace. A good option is the basic three-way switch, which gives you the ability to turn a light or group of lights on or off from two

Big and Dim

Because of the size of high-wattage dimmers, they cannot fit into an ordinary bank of wall switches. Instead, they have to be mounted separately to give them enough room for the cooling fins both to fit and to function properly.

or more points. You could have a switch by the main entrance that controls the main overhead lighting, and a similar one by the entrance to the garage or mudroom. That way, you can turn the lights both on and off as you walk through.

Another important element in a kitchen is the dimmer switch. Rather than a kitchen lighting system that's always on bright, dimmer switches can help to create moods that you need. With an eat-in kitchen, for instance, you might want to have bright lights while you're preparing food, then tone them down during the meal for a different atmosphere. It's as much of a relief to the cook as to the others to have softer light.

Dimmer switches come in a variety of styles, including the classic rheostat, which is the classic round dimmer switch, and new computerized touch pads. My favorite, however, are the simple preset dimmers that have a small slide that adjusts with your fingernail. When the light is flicked on, it shines at the level you set previously. This lets you adjust everything in your home so that it is consistent when you turn the lights on—you won't have to be fumbling and fiddling around to try and reach the right lighting level.

Keep in mind that all dimmer switches are specifically rated for specific fixtures. The standard dimmer is 600 watts. Which means that the total wattage for all the lightbulbs connected to this dimmer switch cannot exceed 600. Even if not overloaded, dimmers do get warm to the touch, which alarms some people. This should be expected, however. Dimmers function by slowing down the electricity that comes full blast at them, much the way Hoover Dam reduces the flow of water. Dimmers rated higher than 600 watts have a built-in cooler system to help reduce the heat buildup. The trim plates around the dimmers actually have a set of aluminum fins cut into them, which allow air to flow in and cool them down.

Now let's turn from the smallest electrical items in the kitchen to the largest ones: the ventilation systems and major appliances.

chapter SIX

Mechanical Inclinations
A ventilation system and major appliances form the mechanical core of the kitchen.

Some years ago, a woman called to have me take a look at her kitchen. She and her family had lived there for about two years, and the kitchen had been renovated within the last decade. It looked nice enough at a quick glance, but a faint yet terrible smell permeated the air. The odor lay somewhere between rancid grease and old food, but no one could locate exactly where it came from. Clearly, this was a case for Sherlock Fix-It.

Looking around the kitchen, I found a single clue as to what was causing the foul smell. Above the stove, there was an exhaust hood and fan, as there should be. Where the fan connected to the back wall, however, grease seemed to be condensing for some reason and dripping back down the backsplash. "I turn the fan on whenever I cook, but I do have to wipe the backsplash down every few days because the grease starts to drip," admitted the woman, who apparently thought this was routine. "Do you think there's anything wrong here?"

Well, I certainly did, but I couldn't believe how elementary this problem would turn out to be. A ventilation system takes fumes and grease generated from cooking and whisks them through the fan and outside of the house, where they escape harmlessly into the air. The fact that grease was dripping on the backsplash meant something different, however. It meant that instead of venting outside, the air and grease were blowing directly against the backsplash and staying there. There wasn't any ventilation going on here at all. Which meant that the previous contractor had forgotten to run a hole through the wall so that the fan could vent to the outside. True, this is Contracting 101, but this contractor obviously never made it past Contracting 100. When I pulled off the vent to take a look I discovered there was no exhaust system. Instead, there was just a fan slapping grease against the backsplash, which would drip down again to the stove in an endless cycle of disgust. While I wouldn't repeat the exact words I uttered when I discovered this mess, they were pretty much synonymous with "Ew, gross!"

Ventilation is one of those things that few homeowners think of first when it comes to redoing their kitchen. Yet it forms an essential component of the mechanical aspects of the kitchen. Along with large appliances, a ventilation system is one of the major factors that distinguishes

a kitchen in the twenty-first century from a kitchen in the nineteenth century. Understanding these elements as you're installing them, rather than years after they *should* have been installed, will help you create a workhorse kitchen that never fails.

Venting Off

During a kitchen renovation, homeowners wrestle with weighty issues when it comes to appliances—like whether that $1,500 European dishwasher really does a better job on the breakfast dishes than that $400 job from GE. This thinking is backward, however, because the real first question when it comes to thinking about the mechanics of a kitchen is whether the ventilation system works well.

Venting is crucial in a kitchen, and this has nothing to do with keeping a house cool and warm. Instead, it has to do with whisking away the odors, grease, and, most of all, the moisture that abounds. Boil a few pots of pasta water, and you can release a gallon or more of water into your home each day. While you might think this "humidifies" the air, there's a distinct problem with this. Moisture pouring into the air in the kitchen accumulates in the room, condenses against windows, and literally begins to drip as it condenses into the insulation in the walls. The result can be mildew, mold, and decay—none of which will contribute to your kitchen's longevity.

Another factor to consider is the grease that is produced in the average kitchen. Unless you dine exclusively on steamed tofu, this is an inevitable problem. Fry up a pound of bacon, however, and you know firsthand all about the mess that splattered grease makes. What you don't necessarily see is the vaporized grease, however. If you've ever cleaned out the filter in a kitchen vent system (and if you haven't, I'd certainly recommend it) you'll find one of the foulest environments imaginable. Fortunately, in a house with a well-tuned vent system, this mess is confined to the filter. In a house where the vent system is substandard, this mess ends up splattered all around the kitchen instead. You literally

Cleaning the Grease Filters

Most of a kitchen can be kept clean with sponging, some vacuuming, and an occasional swabbing of the decks. One area needs something more: the grease filter in the ventilation system. There's probably no part of your home that will become quite as messy.

Cleaning these filters, which are a blend of stainless steel and other metals, is more than just a matter of good household hygiene, however. Grease and dirt accumulating on them can actually become a fire hazard. Before you know it, they can flare up—like some flaming cherries jubilee. Ordinary dishwashing soap barely makes a dent in the grime. The approach I use is to take the filters and run them through the dishwasher once and probably twice. Then I use a cleanser called Grease Magnet around the inside perimeter of the exhaust hood.

Let it soak here for a few minutes, and the grime wipes away. This is something you should probably do three or four times a year— maybe even monthly if you're someone who cooks a great deal.

end up coating every surface in the kitchen with an imperceptible layer of bacon grease combined with everything else you cook. The result is a vile dust magnet, and something that resembles those science projects that try to re-create the conditions upon which life began on Earth. A well-functioning ventilation system can tame this.

An additional benefit from having a fan in place is to vent hot cooking air in the summertime, which can easily overheat the house.

While this doesn't act as an air-conditioning system, it can do its part to help keep your home comfortable.

Too often homeowners leave all aspects of the ventilation system to a contractor, and trust that it will be taken care of satisfactorily. As my friend with the fan that vented to nowhere discovered, it

Common Scents

In addition to removing moisture, heat, and grease from the air, kitchen fans help to manage cooking odors. Without a proper fan and ventilation system, a kitchen will retain a smell that makes the room feel unkempt, no matter how much you try to scrub it clean.

is essential that you take a more active role. Let's begin with a few basics. Ventilation systems have evolved greatly over the decades. The earliest systems, other than an exterior door left ajar, involved nothing more than noisy fans built into the wall. You'd pull on a chain, and the fan would turn on and force air outside. These weren't very efficient, which is why your grandparents' kitchen was more than likely painted with high-gloss paint on the walls. This way, your grandmother could wipe down all the grease that accumulated and splattered against the wall. Effective, yes, but not likely to make the pages of *House Beautiful*.

The first advance came with the advent of the overhead exhaust fan hood. This is basically a metal shroud that fits in between a couple of cabinets that hover over the top of the stove. These first fans did a better job of exhausting heat and odor out of the home, but again, they were quite noisy. In the 1970s, when the microwave oven became popular, the combination exhaust hood/microwave oven fit the same space and became one of the hottest items to own. You can still find them in all different finishes, from black to stainless steel, and for smaller kitchens they make a lot of sense. The fans usually move about 300 cubic feet of air per minute, which is adequate for a small kitchen.

Regardless of the type of fan, there is one cardinal rule. If you're going to put one in, make sure it exhausts. This means it has to connect

A Remote Fan

One common problem with exhaust fans in the kitchen has nothing to do with the fans. Instead, it has to do with the homeowners. They never turn the fans on. Part of this has to do with the noise of the fans, which can be distracting even among so called low-noise devices. One solution to this is to install a "remote" fan. This powerful fan is usually located on the outside of the house, where it can whir away without bothering anyone. Remote fans are found in most restaurants. Go into your favorite hot-dog stand and you'll see a gigantic shroud over the cooking area, but you don't hear the fan—that's because it's mounted up on the roof. This is not a new-fangled contraption at all; it's been in commercial use for decades. Although this involves many additional feet of pipe in the vent system, the systems are still efficient because larger fans that move a greater volume of air can be used.

The residential fans are typically rated anywhere from 600 to 1,000 cubic feet per minute. These fans are more expensive than conventional systems—a typical price might be $1,000 and up compared to $100. But the cost will be more than worth it if it means the fan will actually be turned on.

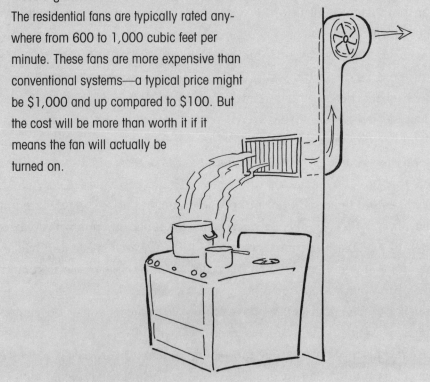

to piping that runs to an exterior wall. Many times, builders—especially in apartments—don't want to spend the extra time and money to install the piping. Instead, they install fans that recirculate the air back into the room, which makes absolutely no sense whatsoever. While this filters the air in a general sort of way, it certainly is not an air-cleansing system. No HEPA filter here! Instead, all it does is take air at a rate of 300 cubic feet per minute from one part of the kitchen and blows it back in your face, usually with the addition of a foul odor from running the air through that grease-lined system. In my view this is actually worse than having no vent system at all. It certainly doesn't help cool the kitchen in the summer, since it just recirculates the heat around the room rather than removing it.

Adding a Vent System

If you're building a kitchen in an addition or in a new house, the task of installing piping for the vent system is easy. Once the room is framed, it's simply set in place before the drywall is attached. But how do you run piping in a house that's already up, without smashing the walls to bits? That's a far greater challenge.

The first thing to keep in mind is that the shorter the pipe is, the more efficient the fan will be. This makes logical sense: If you have a fan pushing air through a straight, 5-foot run, it will operate fairly well. Take that same fan and place it at the end of an 80-foot tangle with a bunch of right-angle turns, however, and you'll barely feel a puff at the outflow. Now comes the piping material itself. Many people assume that vent pipes for the kitchen can be the same as the flexible vinyl tubes attached to dryers—you know, the ones that look like giant Slinkies. No way. Instead, the pipe embedded in the walls should be rigid galvanized metal, and not simply an aluminum-skinned version of the vinyl Slinky. It looks like a stovepipe. Laying this out in a new kitchen is easy enough, but in an existing kitchen the challenge becomes obvious. Planning the course is essential to success.

Down with Downdraft Vents?

In a kitchen, you need two things: a stove and a vent above it to draw away grease, odors, and heat. One common method of dealing with this involves combining the two, in the form of a stove that has a downdraft vent between the burners. This is designed to eliminate the need for an overhead vent, both for looks and for the expense and for the needed room, especially in an island. The downdraft vent is supposed to suck the vapors away, and while this seems like a good idea, in my opinion, it doesn't work very well in practice—especially with gas stoves. The problem is that the vent is needed most when the flame is on high. But the vent pulls the flame, too, and greatly reduces its heating capacity. By pulling the flame, it can lead to hot spots when you cook. For example, if you're making an omelet, you'll burn one half and not the other. In addition, the venting power of these fans is fairly small. Add a couple of boiling pots to the stuff—especially tall ones—and the downdraft vent does practically nothing.

A better solution has emerged in recent years, which I think is a big improvement on ordinary downdraft vents. In these, a vent actually rises up from the back of the stove, with the press of a button. It literally slides up like a sash in a double-hung window. At the top edge is an open vent, which pulls in odors with the help of a small yet powerful fan inside. This system seems to have a more powerful draw than the classic down vent. Plus, since it's raised up in the air, it doesn't pull the flame in quite the same way.

One common way of hiding the piping is by working it up from the fan and out through the top of the wall near the ceiling. Then it lines up with the spaces between lumber in the ceiling and runs to the nearest outside wall. The challenge comes in trying to conceal the pipe in the visible area in the kitchen. If you have conventional 8-foot ceilings, that task is made fairly easy because the upper wall cabinets tend to run all the way up to the ceiling. The pipe can actually be cut and positioned so that it runs through one of the upper cabinets. This conceals it from view—except when you open the cabinet. To avoid that "hillbilly" look, I always box in the pipe with wood that matches the exterior of the cabinet. This way, it's completely hidden. With taller ceiling heights, the cabinets tend to hang between 12 and 24 inches below the ceiling. In this case, the pipe will run straight up from the tops. I enclose the area with drywall and paint it the same color as the wall, so you won't even notice it.

Where the pipe reaches the outside wall, a 6-inch-diameter hole typically has to be drilled right through the side of the house. (Some larger residential fans require an 8-inch or even a 12-inch diameter hole). This is something that often makes people shudder, since they think their house has been ruined. The way kitchen vents are piped and connected to the outside wall is critical to how well they work, and how well they keep drafts from going back into the house. Most of them come with internal dampers that control drafts near the fan, but the shroud or the housing that sits on the outside of the house also has a damper to keep wintry winds from passing through the vent into the house.

Keep in mind that in very cold climates, additional

Need Title

If you're forced to run ductwork of substantial length, try to avoid any 90-degree turns. These drastically reduce the efficiency of the fan, and also become collectors of dirt and grease. Instead, ease the flow by using two 45-degree angle pipes. Another way to maintain efficiency is to increase the size of the blower motor.

Old Appliances Made New

One of the hot trends in appliances these days is the retro look—curvy refrigerators, and stoves that look like they came out of the Herbert Hoover White House. These can add a great style, but there's a way you can get the same look for a fraction of the cost: by finding the original and restoring it.

I wouldn't necessarily recommend buying an old refrigerator or dishwasher that hasn't already been restored, because upgrading one and adding a new motor would cost far more than buying something new. But old stoves are a different matter. Renovating a New York City apartment, my friend Gina came home to find the contractors hauling the old 1930s stove out. "Wait a minute, put that back," she said. And with a lot of cleaning, E-Z-Off, and a few delicate swipes with a razor blade to remove eighty years of paint and what I would charitably call "gunk," she came up with a beauty. The great thing about old stoves is that there are very few movable or breakable parts. They may not "convect" along with the super-heated convection ovens, but they will do the job—and look great in the process.

A few places to look on the Internet are on e-Bay, as well as classicappliances.com, where you can also advertise for needed parts. Another Web site is antiqueappliances.com, which sells both restored and unrestored equipment. A 1926 Oriole gas stove, which looks something like a cross between an old Singer sewing machine and a camping stove, recently sold for $2,995, which included shipping anywhere in the United States. Pricey, perhaps, but it's something you can guarantee the neighbors sure won't have. Or check out local newspaper ads, flea markets, and estate sales. They may have a great appliance and not even imagine that anyone would want it.

precautions have to be taken to keep the vent from turning into an Arctic air conditioner. Metal conducts cold, as well as heat, but it is the cold that will be most noticeable. The metal housing chills on the outside, then passes this along the rigid metal tube to the inside. It creates a terrific draft, almost like having a fan on that blows the outdoor air inside—even with the damper firmly in place. The trick to prevent this is to create a break point in the metal pipe, which is literally a gap made of vinyl or nylon that clips into place near the outside connection so that metal does not touch metal. This radically slows the transference of cold and reduces drafts.

Choosing Appliances

As with everything else, we often shop for major appliances—the refrigerator, the dishwasher, the stove—by their looks alone. Does the refrigerator have style? Does the dishwasher look sleek? Is that stove making a bold design statement? Sure, looks are an element to consider, but the more important aspect to consider is how well they work and whether you're getting your money's worth.

For those of us who grew up in a kitchen whose appliances were limited to a stove and a refrigerator and maybe a dishwasher, the lineup of today's possibilities is dazzling indeed—including wine coolers, icemakers, trash compactors, and even warming drawers. Sorting through the range of possibilities is a little like choosing the options on a new car. There are useful things, such as power windows, and gimmicks, such as heated seats, that may be of interest only to some and not to others. The same is true of kitchen appliances. There are good-quality ovens and cooktops that can handle any recipe, and then there are specialty items such as glass ceramic surfaces that work by a process called "magnetic-induction," which seem to have more to do with giving you bragging rights than improving the quality of the food you cook. One over-the-top European stove, produced by Aga, runs twenty-four hours a day with burners set at different temperatures for all cooking needs—roasting, toasting, boiling, braising, steaming, stewing, simmering, frying, grilling, and keeping food warm. The cost? Between $10,000 and $13,000, which could probably pay for all of your appliances a few times over. You can buy an ordinary refrigerator that chills things just fine; or, you can buy a refrigerator with a moisture-sensing device called a humidistat, spill-proof shelves, and a door that beeps when it is left ajar. You can find appliances that easily plunk into standard-sized holes and nooks built into the cabinets. Or, you can spend thousands of dollars more to create an invisible look in which the appliances appear built in. Deciding what you want in advance can save a great deal in time and money.

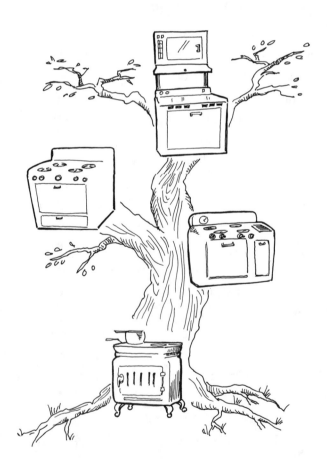

The first step in shopping for appliances is to avoid being brand-conscious. When you shop for a car, one of the first things you realize is how similar certain models are. Some Japanese models, for instance, have nearly identical American-made counterparts that cost less. This is also true with appliances, since many brands are owned by the same small group of manufacturers. The result is a family tree more entwined than the House of Hapsburg. Take Electrolux Home Products, for instance. No longer confined to vacuum cleaners, this company now produces Frigidaire, Tappan, and White-Westinghouse. Maytag developed its own brand years ago—who could forget the lonely Maytag repairman? Since then, Maytag has branched out. It now produces Jenn-Air, Amana, and Magic Chef. Sub-Zero? They make great refrigerators, and recently acquired the Wolf Appliance Company, as well. And the obscure sounding BSH Home Appliances Corporation produces appliances under the brand names Bosch, Thermador, and Gagganau. Whirlpool, for its part, sells its products as Kitchen Aid, Bauknecht, Roper, Inglis, and Speed Queen.

The way to begin searching for appliances is with a list. First, write down a description of how you cook, shop for food, and entertain. If you've got a swirling social life, love to cook, and have more children than the Waltons, then think big. Two dishwashers—which is actually a trend in high-end kitchens—might make practical sense for an intensively used kitchen, as a way of keeping on top of the mess. A giant refrigerator-freezer can be just the item needed if you buy in bulk and freeze seasonal food for use throughout the year. And if you're always at the stove (and I do mean always), then maybe you do need a stove that knows the precise temperature differences between braising and stewing. On the other hand, if your idea of cooking involves slicing some cheese to put on a few crackers and cracking open a six-pack of yogurt, then your five-figure investment in luxury appliances is going to turn into the worst and dustiest investment you ever made. When you've made your list, the next step is to decide on your budget for major appliances, and stick to it. Sure, go get a giant Sub-Zero refrigerator—after all, I did—but pair it with a lower-cost stove and a dishwasher from different manufacturers that match in style but not in price. Going pricey on one appliance doesn't mean you have to go pricey on them all.

Too often, with appliances and in fact every other aspect of a kitchen, we're trying to make a statement—without tempering that with what we can afford, or with what makes practical sense. I have a friend, for instance, and had he made a list of his cooking needs, he would have realized that the microwave was probably his greatest companion in life. He uses it for everything from reheating leftovers to cooking popcorn. Yet in redesigning his kitchen, he tried to achieve a "streamlined" look, and, amazingly, left the microwave out. "I wanted a serious kitchen, and it just didn't belong—it was too conspicuous," he said. A few months later, serious or not, he went out and bought a microwave, which is now perched in the center of the island, where it looks about as streamlined as Mt. Rushmore.

Putting It All Together

With all of the ingredients of a great kitchen in hand, let's take a final look at the process of assembling one in your home.

Unless you've been, say, Norm Abram in a previous life, this inevitably involves working with a contractor. While our relationship with our home is largely an emotional one, as anyone who has agonized while house hunting or counted the days to a real estate closing well knows, our relationship with a contractor should be all business. Many home-owners quickly forget this, however. They mistakenly believe that a con-tractor will fall in love with their home and the project, and make heroic efforts to bring things together beautifully, and under budget. As with all romantic notions, this one fails more often than not. Worse than disillu-sionment, however, is the fact that homeowners are sometimes so grate-ful to have a contractor begin the work that they fail to take the precautions necessary to guarantee that the work will be finished correctly. This is like

Up to Code

Some years ago, I renovated a kitchen in a suburb of Chicago. It was a lavish job, to be sure, but the homeowner wanted to put her money into the things that could be seen, rather than the electrical wiring that lay behind it. The house had 100-amp service—which was barely adequate for most homes—but she was not willing to spend a few thousand dollars more and upgrade to 200-amp service. The kitchen looked terrific, but the massive draw from all the new appliances left the house flickering like a Christmas tree whenever the lights came on.

Updated electrical wiring is essential to any kitchen renovation because today's appliances draw so much power. In addition, many major appliances need their own dedicated circuit, such as the refrigerator, the dishwasher, and even the garbage disposal, if you have one. Separate circuits prevent your home's electrical system from overloading, and reduce the risk of fire as well as power outages. Installing these is a job for a *licensed electrician* only. You can't cut corners here by slapping new outlets into ancient wiring systems. If you do, you'll simply have to spend more money in the future to rewire everything the right way—and will have to rip up parts of your newly renovated kitchen in order to do it.

My friend with the 100-amp service found this out the hard way. After living with an annoying and dangerous electrical system, she paid thousands more than she needed to for upgraded electrical service. By this time, however, she opted for overkill: 300-amp service, which is probably enough to light a baseball field. Still, she can be sure she'll never have flickering lights again.

Garbage Disposals

For those of you who read my first book, feel free to skip this continuation of my diatribe against what I consider to be one of the sloppiest and most wasteful inventions in history. Yes, I'm referring to the garbage disposal.

I do not have a garbage disposal in my home, and I am going to take this a step further by saying I do not think you should have a garbage disposal in your home, either. While they seem to be the most convenient devices—you just chuck stuff in there, flick a switch, and it's gone forever—the opposite is true. For one thing, all that ground up gunk (most of which could have been composted) ends up flushed into the overloaded city sewer system or into your easily clogged septic tank. Second, these things inevitably break down. However sturdy the motor, there is only so much it can take in the battle against a chicken bone, a peach pit, or, as a friend of mine recently discovered, an heirloom silver ladle from his grandmother's family that accidentally slipped into the drain. Yikes!

Life in the kitchen should be focused on simplifying things, not by adding gadgets of dubious benefit that will eventually break down and require fixing. A better solution is the sink strainer, which is 99 percent effective at catching debris in the sink.

trying to bake a cake by whipping up all the ingredients, then forgetting to turn the oven on: You'll end up with a mess that is never finished.

The bond between the contractor and the homeowner is built on trust, and a degree of friendship and respect is essential as the project progresses. But there are some specific things you can do to guarantee that trust won't just evaporate, or that friendship won't fly out the window when the budget is exceeded by 50 percent. For a homeowner, the first

Stainless Steel's Tarnished Truth

Yes, they call it stainless steel. No, it sure doesn't seem it when put to use. Stainless steel panels are increasingly popular on appliances because of their streamlined, modern look. Yet while stainless steel may not actually rust or corrode, it will show signs of abuse, including scratch marks, smudges, and fingerprints.

One solution is to buy stainless-steel cleaner and use it regularly to keep the surface fresh looking. This is a fairly high-maintenance surface, and needs to be cleaned weekly, and even daily in a household with young children. The cleaner leaves behind a slightly oily coating that helps keep fingerprints away. One tip: Stainless steel tends to be brushed and therefore has a grain. If you clean with the grain, you minimize the scratches that etch into the surface over time. If you swirl at random, however, you're going to add to them.

Despite the work required to keep stainless steel looking good, I love the look. A great stainless-steel refrigerator or stove can easily become the focal point for a kitchen, in a way no almond-colored appliance ever will. In addition, stainless-steel appliances hold up; they'll look as good twenty years from now as they do today—as long as you put in the effort required to keep them clean.

way to guarantee a good relationship with a contractor is to be willing to pay a fair price for the work being done in the first place. The real problems begin to brew when homeowners try to get a bargain. If you choose your contractors simply by taking the lowest bid, you deserve as much blame as they do when the project flops. Instead, find a contractor by asking friends and family for recommendations, check references, and go to see in person other projects the contractor has done. Above all, be willing to wait. If you like a person's work, then the fact that it takes three, four, five, and even six months to be worked into their schedule should be considered a reasonable part of the process. People willingly wait months to schedule an appointment with a dentist that they trust, yet too often they become pushy and impatient when waiting for a good contractor.

Once you've selected someone you can work with, the key to ensuring a smooth flow of the project is to enforce a strict payment schedule and weekly updates about any cost overruns. Don't ever pay for any portion of the project until it is completed to your satisfaction. Some contractors, especially small ones, might ask for an up-front payment; in all cases, resist it. What's to keep them from walking away with your money before you've gotten anything? Nothing. For small jobs, pay for the work only when it is completed. For larger kitchen renovations, agree to a payment schedule—but again, only make payments for the work that is actually completed.

Finally, schedule a weekly meeting with the contractor to go over receipts. Friday is probably the best day for this. Make sure the contractor asks your approval for any unbudgeted expenses and gives you a weekly accounting of any cost overruns. You don't want any surprises at the end, when you discover that those few little changes you made in the configuration of the cabinets have ended up costing you $2,500 more.

As we've seen, a kitchen is a room to be molded to the way you live, and not some showpiece to be tailored to other people's tastes and other people's lifestyles. Choose every element of it—including the contractor—according to what makes the best practical sense for you. Trust me, the result will be a kitchen that cooks.

Appendix

appendix

Essential Resources

Not sure where to turn to find out
more about your kitchen-to-be?
Let the journey begin here.

When you're planning a kitchen, information isn't everything—it's the

only thing. The more you find out about materials and installation tech-

niques and appliances that are available, the more you can turn this to

your advantage in crafting the kitchen that suits you best. No list of

resources will ever be complete, but I've narrowed down the possibilities

to include some that I rely on that I know will help get you started. Where

they exist, I've included phone numbers, but try the Web sites first. You'll

save time, and probably find everything you need without having to wait

for the mail to arrive.

American Council for an Energy-Efficient Economy

www.aceee.org
1001 Connecticut Avenue, NW
Suite 801
Washington, DC 20036
202-429-0063

Search this Web site for information on electrical use of appliances, including a listing of energy-efficient refrigerators.

American Institute of Architects

www.aia.org
1735 New York Avenue, NW
Washington, DC 20006
800-AIA-3837

Use this Web site to find books and design resources, as well as a licensed architect to help turn your kitchen dreams into a workable plan.

American Lighting Association

www.americanlightingassoc.com
P.O. Box 420288
Dallas, TX 75342
800-274-4484

Look on the Web site under "lighting tips and information" for pointers on kitchen lighting; spend $5, and get a booklet on tips for lighting the whole house.

American Society of Interior Designers

www.asid.org

608 Massachusetts Avenue, NE

Washington, DC 20002

202-546-3480

For a list of licensed interior designers in your area, start here; also includes tips on how to work with one once you've hired him or her.

Association of Home Appliance Manufacturers

www.aham.org

1111 19th Street, NW

Suite 402

Washington, DC 20036

202-872-5955

Look under the "just for consumers" section for tips about everything from prolonging the life of electrical appliances to avoiding microwave "boil-overs."

Better Homes and Gardens magazine

www.bhg.com

Meredith Corporation

1716 Locust Street

Des Moines, IA 50309-3023

Search this Web site under "kitchen" to find volumes of information about how to plan a kitchen and choose materials.

Color Marketing Group

www.colormarketing.org

5904 Richmond Highway

#408

Alexandria, VA 22303

703-329-8500

On this entertaining Web site, you can learn about such things as forecasting color trends and the history of color—from basic black to today's iridescent effects.

DoItYourself.Com

www.doityourself.com

Find answers to kitchen questions on this Web site, including how to use a home equity loan, how to dismantle an old kitchen, and how to install a hood vent system.

Hometime.Com

www.hometime.com

The Web site for this popular TV show is a great how-to source for kitchen projects you can tackle yourself—along with a resource guide for books, videos, and manufacturers.

Home Ventilating Institute

www.hvi.org

30 W. University Drive

Arlington Heights, IL 60004

847-394-0150

If ventilation is the topic you're interested in, this Web site is the one for you—filled with detailed information, scientific studies, and product suggestions.

HowStuffWorks.Com

www.howstuffworks.com

Want to know the nuts and bolts of what makes a refrigerator run or how a microwave actually cooks? Look no further than this authoritative Web site.

International Association of Lighting Designers

www.iald.org
Suite 9-104
The Merchandise Mart
Chicago, IL 60654
312-527-3677

Designed for the building trade, this Web site contains everything you could possibly want to know about lighting—as well as tips for working with lighting designers.

Kitchen and Bath Business magazine

www.kitchen-bath.com
VNU eMedia, Inc.
770 Broadway, 6th Floor
New York, NY 10003

This Web site contains a useful question-and-answer section about kitchen renovation, as well as detailed how-to articles, such as how to strip paint off old cabinets.

Kitchen and Bath Design News magazine

www.kbdn.net
Cygnus Business Media
1233 Janesville Avenue
Fort Atkinson, WI 53538

Sponsored by a leading magazine for designers, this Web site contains useful tips—such as a primer on glass tiles—as well as buyers' guides for everything in the kitchen.

Kitchen Cabinet Manufacturers Association

www.kcma.org
1899 Preston White Drive
Reston, VA 20191-5435
703-264-1690

Designed for cabinet manufacturers, this Web site can help you select cabinets, as well as steer you toward manufacturers and dealers.

Kitchen-Design.Com

www.kitchen-design.com

This engaging and interactive Web site allows you to design a kitchen in terms of layout and décor, with assistance from a French designer.

Kitchens.Com

www.kitchens.com

On this Web site, learn about new products and approaches to kitchen renovations, and search for décor recommendations based on the style of your house.

National Fire Protection Association

www.nfpa.org
1 Batterymarch Park
Quincy, MA 02269
800-344-3555/617-770-3000

Do a search on this Web site to learn about how to use a fire extinguisher, as well as to download a tip sheet on improving fire safety in the kitchen.

National Kitchen & Bath Association

www.nkba.org
687 Willow Grove Street
Hackettstown, NJ 07840
877-NKBA-PRO (843-6522)

This comprehensive Web site includes tips from the pros, an ideas section, and a gallery of real kitchens, as well as the stories behind them.

Wallcoverings Association

www.wallcoverings.org
401 N. Michigan Avenue
Chicago, IL 60611
312-644-6610

Click on this Web site to learn the basics of wallpapering, including a do-it-yourself guide, information on styles of wallpaper, as well as wallpaper history.

Water Quality Association

www.wqa.org

4151 Naperville Road

Lisle, IL 60532

630-505-0160

To diagnose water problems, head to this Web site; includes information on contaminants from arsenic to zinc, foul odors, and mineral deposits.

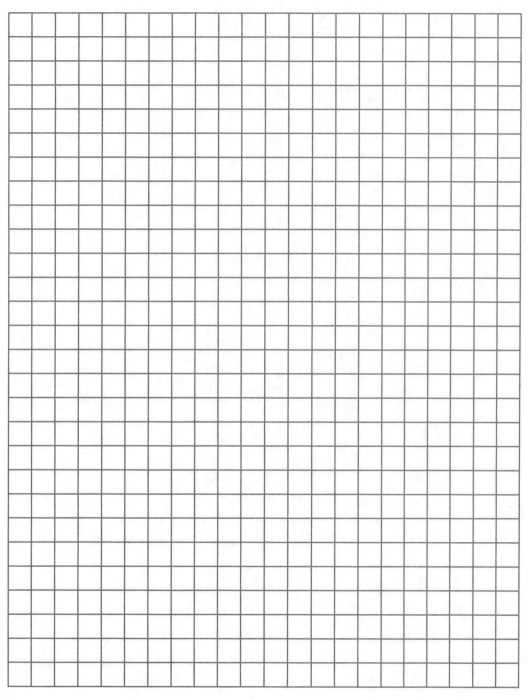

Scale: 1/4″ to a foot

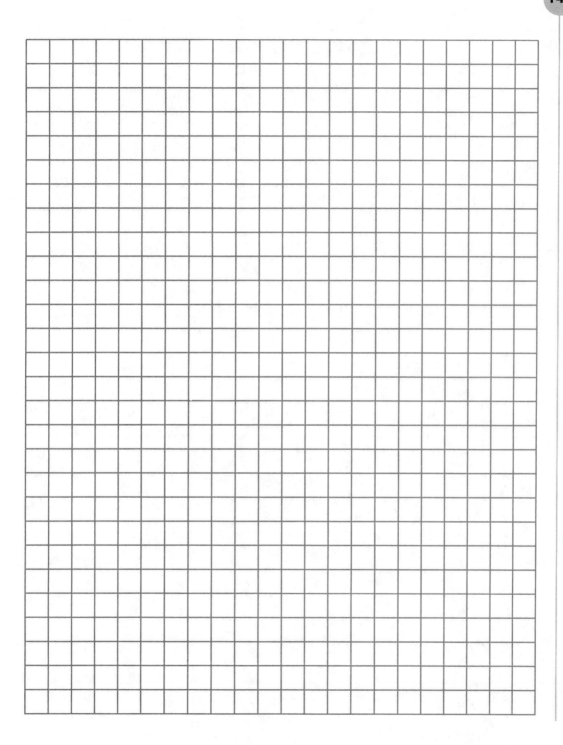

About the Authors

Lou Manfredini started working in a hardware store when he was thirteen years old. He worked as a carpenter's apprentice in college and opened his own construction company in Chicago in 1985. His media career began ten years later when he pitched the idea of a call-in show to a local radio station. WGN-AM picked up the show, and Mr. Fix-It was born. The radio show is now nationally syndicated, and Lou is also a frequent contributor to television and print media, as well. He appears regularly on the *Today Show,* and has a bimonthly column in *USA Weekend.* He still runs his own construction company, and actively builds and renovates homes. Lou lives in Chicago with his wife and four children.

Curtis Rist, an award-winning journalist and author, began his home improvement career a decade ago when he attended house building school, then designed and helped construct his own house. He is former senior writer at *This Old House* magazine and the coauthor of the *This Old House Homeowner's Manual.* Inspired by working with Lou on their first book, *House Smarts,* he began a new career as a contractor—and now buys and renovates old houses in Hudson, New York, where he lives with his wife and two sons.

Shower in a stylish room —without taking a bath

- Create an elegant-looking bathroom without an exorbitant price tag

- Learn to hang like a pro, from towel racks to shower curtains

- Give your bathroom plenty of light— even if there's no window

- Add necessary storage to your bathroom—without the clutter

- Understand the basics of plumbing and say good-bye to drips

- Discover which projects require expert assistance—and which you can handle yourself

- Avoid pitfalls and ask your contractor the right questions

- Accentuate your room with unique fixtures and finishing touches

Includes illustrations, anecdotes, specific prices, essential tips, and a lifetime of insight

Lou Manfredini's **BATH SMARTS**

Make over your bathroom with minimum fuss

Save thousands of dollars with handy homebuilders' secrets

Expert advice on "do it yourself" projects

Learn when to get a contractor, and at the lowest cost

LOU MANFREDINI
Columnist for *USA WEEKEND* Magazine and *Today* show contributor

WITH CURTIS RIST

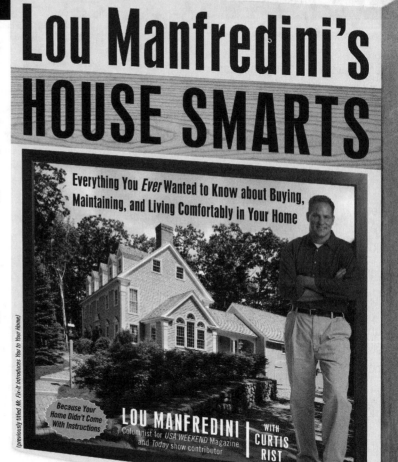